Beautiful & pointless

Beautiful

&

pointless

{ *A Guide to Modern Poetry* }

DAVID ORR

HARPER ● PERENNIAL

NEW YORK • LONDON • TORONTO • SYDNEY • NEW DELHI • AUCKLAND

HARPER ● PERENNIAL

An extension of this copyright page appears on pages 197–200.

A hardcover edition of this book was published in 2011 by HarperCollins Publishers.

BEAUTIFUL & POINTLESS. Copyright © 2011 by David Orr. All rights reserved.
Printed in the United States of America. No part of this book may be used or reproduced
in any manner whatsoever without written permission except in the case of brief
quotations embodied in critical articles and reviews. For information address
HarperCollins Publishers, 10 East 53rd Street, New York, NY 10022.

HarperCollins books may be purchased for educational, business, or sales promotional
use. For information please write: Special Markets Department,
HarperCollins Publishers, 10 East 53rd Street, New York, NY 10022.

FIRST HARPER PERENNIAL EDITION PUBLISHED 2012.

Designed by Leah Carlson-Stanisic

The Library of Congress has catalogued the hardcover edition as follows:

Orr, David.
    Beautiful & pointless : a guide to modern poetry / David Orr.— 1st ed.
      p.   cm.
    ISBN 978-0-06-167345-0
    1. Poetry. I. Title. II. Title: Beautiful and pointless.
PN1031.O77 2011
808.1—dc22

                                                              2011011599

ISBN 978-0-06-167346-7 (pbk.)

12 13 14 15 16   OV/RRD   10 9 8 7 6 5 4 3 2 1

For my family

contents

introduction

THIS BOOK IS ABOUT modern poetry. But a book about modern poetry can't be as confidently "about" its subject as a book about, say, college football or soap operas or dog shows or the pastas of Northern Italy. That's because poetry is *poetry*—it supposedly comes to us wrapped in mystery, veiled in shadow, cloaked in doubt, swaddled in . . . well, you get the idea. Consequently, the potential audience for a book about poetry nowadays consists of two mutually uncomprehending factions: the poets, for whom poetry is a matter of casual, day-to-day conversation; and the rest of the world, for whom it's a subject of at best mild and confused interest.

This has all been said before. For decades now, one of the poetry world's favorite activities has been bemoaning its lost audience, then bemoaning the bemoaning, then bemoaning that bemoaning, until finally everyone shrugs and applies for a grant from the National Endowment for the Arts. Typically, because these are poetry readers we're talking about, the titles of these lamentations and counter-lamentations are masterstrokes of stoic understatement. Like:

"Who Killed Poetry?" (Joseph Epstein, 1988)

"Death to the Death of Poetry" (Donald Hall, 1989)

Can Poetry Matter? (Dana Gioia, 1991)

After the Death of Poetry (Vernon Shetley, 1993)

"Dead or Alive? Poetry at Risk" (Stephen Goode, 1993)

"Why Poetry Is Dying" (J. S. Salemi, 2001)

"Poetry Is Dead. Does Anybody Really Care?" (Bruce Wexler, 2003)

No matter which side the author happens to favor, the discussion tends to take on a weirdly personal tenor, as if poetry were a bedridden grandmother whose every sniffle was being evaluated for incipient pneumonia. And as with most potential deathbed scenes, the mood among the gathered family wavers between self-satisfied moralizing and an embattled, panicky vigilance.

This book is not concerned with that debate—or at least, not with the usual terms of that debate. It will not focus on events that may or may not have occurred ninety years ago that may or may not have lost an audience that poetry may or may not have possessed; nor will it attempt to determine whether poetry is dead or alive, comatose or just feeling a little woozy. Poetry may be any or all or none of those things. In the end, however, such arguments are interesting only to (some) poets, and to paraphrase Emerson, you can't see a field when you're standing in the middle of it. Instead, this book will focus on the relationship that exists—right now, not fifty years ago—between contemporary poetry and general readers, as well as the kind of experiences that such readers can expect from modern writing, if they're given a chance to relate to what they're looking at.

And there's the difficulty. A smart, educated person who likes Charlie Kaufman's movies and tolerates Thomas Pynchon's novels, who works in a job that involves phrases like "amortized debentures" or "easement by estoppel" or "nomological necessity"—that person is often not so much annoyed by poetry as confounded by it. Such a reader doesn't look at a contemporary poem and confidently declare, "I don't like this"; he thinks, "I have no idea what this is . . . maybe I don't like it?" In fact, if more people actively disliked poetry, the news would be much better for poets: When we dislike something, we've at least acknowledged a basis for judgment and an interest in the outcome. What poets have faced for almost half a century, though, is a chasm between their art and the broader culture that's nearly as profound as the divide between land and sea, or sea and air. This is what Randall Jarrell had in mind when he said that "if we were in the habit of reading poets their obscurity would not matter; and, once we are out of the habit, their clarity does not help." The sweetest songs of the dolphins are lost on the gannets.

Nor is that disconnect reduced much by the two primary ways in which contemporary poetry is discussed on the shelves of your local bookstore or library. You might call these approaches the Scholarly Model and the How-to Model. A book written according to the Scholarly Model is exactly what it sounds like—an academic treatise intended to add glitter to a young professor's résumé—and its typical structure runs as follows:

1. Introduction; in which the author makes a general statement about the poetry world, often including some kind of on-the-one-hand-on-the-other discussion of formalism and the avant-garde, neither of which will mean much to anyone without a subscription to *Poetry* magazine;

2. Middle section consisting of three or four chapters devoted to individual poets, one of whom will be John Ashbery; and

3. Conclusion; in which the author argues for more narrative, or more personal detail, or more attention to language itself, or more poets whose names are palindromes, or more poems involving otters, etc.

Books written according to this formula can be hugely enjoyable and smart, but they don't have much to say to the general reader. Even a modern classic like Robert Pinsky's *The Situation of Poetry* is addressing a state of affairs in which its intended audience is already thoroughly situated.

Ironically enough, the How-to books can be even less helpful. These are the volumes with titles like *How to Embrace Poetry* or *Writing Your First Poem* or *Opening Your Heart to Verse* or something equally reminiscent of a do-it-yourself guide to window treatments crossed with a Hallmark card. The problem here is not that such books are written in bad faith or contain inaccurate information; on the contrary, they're among the best intentioned items to be found in a Barnes & Noble, and their documentation of sonnets, sestinas, and iambic trimeter is usually impeccable. The problem is that many good readers don't understand, as a basic matter, how to respond to the art form. As a result, the How-to Model's combination of technical information and platitudes can resemble a golf lesson that consists solely of being told what a nine iron is and how crisp the air can be at St Andrews on a fine September morning, without a single remark about how one actually goes about playing golf. Or to put it another way, the poetry world has been very successful at discussing instruments, classifications, histories, and theories; it's been less successful at conveying what it really means to read poetry, and by extension, why such reading might be as worthwhile as watching the director's cut of *Blade Runner*.

It might therefore help to change our idea of what learning about poetry should be like in the first place. After all, if there's one thing that often unites academic treatments and how-to guides, it's the implicit assumption that relating to poetry is like solving a calculus problem while being zapped with a cattle prod—that is, the dull business of poetic interpretation (". . . and here we have a reference to early Stevens") is coupled uneasily with testimonials announcing poetry's ability to derange the senses, make us lose ourselves in rapture, dance naked under the full moon, and so forth. We seem trapped between a tediously mechanical view of poems and an unjustifiably shamanistic view of poetry itself. If you're a casual reader, then, it's easy to feel that your response to the art is somehow wrong, that you're either insufficiently smart or insufficiently soulful. Any of us may be both those things, of course, but that's an issue that should be resolved after the reader's initial response has been fairly accounted for.

What, then, is that initial response most "like"? When a nonspecialist audience is responding well to a poem, its reaction is a kind of tentative pleasure, a puzzled interest that resembles the affection a traveler bears for a destination that both welcomes and confounds him. For such readers, then, it's not necessarily helpful to talk about poetry as if it were a device to be assembled or a religious experience to be undergone. Rather, it would be useful to talk about poetry as if it were, for example, Belgium.

The comparison may seem ridiculous at first, but consider the way you'd be thinking about Belgium if you were planning a trip there. You might try to learn a few useful phrases, or read a little Belgian history, or thumb through a guidebook in search of museums, restaurants, flea markets, or promising-sounding bars. The important thing is that you'd know you were going to be confused, or at least occasionally at a loss, and you'd accept that confusion as part of the experience. What you wouldn't do, however, is become paralyzed with anxiety because you don't speak fluent Flemish, or convinced that to really "get" Belgium, you need to memorize the Brussels phone book. Nor would you decide in advance that you'd never understand Belgians because you couldn't immediately determine why their most famous public statue is a depiction of a naked kid peeing in a fountain (which is true). You'd probably figure, hey, that's what they like in Belgium; if I stick around long enough, maybe it'll all make sense.

Poetry is best thought of the same way. English verse has existed for nearly a thousand years (more if you count Old English artifacts like *The Dream of the Rood*); it's impossible for most readers to take in even a tenth of the best poetry written in that time, to say nothing of the criticism and translated poems that are equally a part of our poetic heritage. The art form is enormous and perplexing, and at least half of it is of interest only to scholars and the certifiably disturbed. So the best most readers can hope to do is amble across the

landscape, taking time to visit some of the less obvious at-
tractions as well as the racy ones, pausing to nap in a shady
spot or to sample some of the local dishes, even the ones that
smell like wet dog. Like all foreign countries, poetry has
customs and rules that should be respected, but you don't
need to have memorized the entire catalogue of local rituals
in order to make the trip worthwhile. As with a vacation in
Belgium, all you need is a little patience and the motivation
to book your tickets.

This book will try to help you. It will do so not by of-
fering charts, definitions, and representative surveys—such
studies already exist, and you can look them up if you need
them. Instead, this book will try to give you a sense of what
modern poets think about, how those poets talk about what
they're thinking about, and most important, how an indi-
vidual poetry reader relates to the art he usually likes, always
loves, and is frequently annoyed by. Accordingly, each chap-
ter often will be idiosyncratic and unfair. Personal responses
(as opposed to public judgments) are generally both of those
things, and this book is, above all else, an attempt to let you
see how that individual reader—how *I*—read poetry, so
that you might feel better equipped to read it in your own
way for yourself.

This is a quirky project, admittedly, and the book's
structure reflects that fact. You won't find a list of "poets to
read," or for that matter, any chapters or sections covering
individual poets. That isn't because I don't favor particular

writers, but rather because it makes little sense to focus on performers when the real difficulty lies in appreciating the context in which performance occurs. Think of it this way: If you'd never seen a college football game, it wouldn't help much to read an article about the ten greatest wide receivers of all time. But it might help to sit in a bar and listen as a Georgia fan and a Clemson fan discuss a game they'd just been to. At the very least, you'd see what made them happy, what bothered them, what kinds of things they thought were funny, and what experiences seem to have stayed with them through the long ride to the bar and the drink they had before you showed up. You'd get a sense of why the world we call "college football" might be worth visiting.

What follows will be like that conversation. I've arranged the chapters according to concepts that matter in the world of poetry—The Personal, The Political, Form, Ambition, The Fishbowl (which focuses on the sociology of poetry), and Why Bother? (the focus of which should be evident). They aren't the only things that poets think about, of course (nor would my fellow poets agree that our concerns may be so neatly subdivided), but for me, these are topics that allow an interested outsider to understand what poetry readers are talking about when they're talking about poetry. The chapters themselves are loose, anecdotal, occasionally inappropriate, and decidedly candid. I don't expect you to agree with everything that's said in each of them; in fact, I'll go further and say that I hope you don't. If you do, you'll be prevent-

Beautiful & pointless

the personal

POETRY CRITICS ARE OFTEN nervous about being asked what they do for a living. It's not that we don't enjoy our work—we do, mostly—but rather that it can be awkward to explain what a contemporary poetry critic does when many people are surprised to learn that there is such a thing as contemporary poetry in the first place. We're talking, after all, about an art form that currently occupies a position in the popular consciousness somewhere between lute playing and crewel embroidery. But there's another, more important reason that poetry critics are sometimes reluctant to talk about their occupation, and it is probably best demonstrated by an anecdote.

Several years ago, I was at a party filled with nonpoets and was introduced to a friend of a friend. She asked about my job, and I told her that I worked part-time as a book critic. She asked where my pieces usually appeared, and I said *The New York Times Book Review*. At this, she responded, "Oh, that's great!" and began talking about how much she admired book reviewers, authors, and the literary life in general. Then she put her hand on my arm and asked, "And what kind of books do you review?" I was feeling pleased with myself after all the compliments, so I proudly announced, "I'm a poetry critic." She gave me a look as if I'd just tossed a sackful of kittens into a mulcher. "Wait a minute," she said, "you mean you criticize people's *poetry*?"

Because poetry, we're told, is the pure expression of our inner lives. It is the prism through which the soul is glimpsed. It is the spontaneous overflow of powerful feeling. It is the fulfillment of the desire expressed in Corinthians to "know even as also I am known," and a means of answering Pete Townshend's question "Can you see the real me?" To create a poem is to express something central about oneself, and to read poetry is to perceive a writer "as he actually is." Poetry is personal.

Or such, at any rate, is the common belief. Poets themselves are more ambivalent. On one hand, we have T. S. Eliot's famous declaration that "the progress of an artist is a continual self-sacrifice, a continual extinction of personality"; on the other, we have the actual work of T. S. Eliot, which in its nervous avoidance of sentiment can seem almost sentimental. More recently, one can pick up an issue of *Poetry* and find lines like the ones that conclude Randall Mann's "The Fall of 1992":

> Love was a doorknob
> statement, a breakneck goodbye—
> and the walk of shame
> without shame, the hair disheveled, curl
> of Kools, and desolate birds like ampersands . . .
>
> I re-did my face
> in the bar bathroom, above
> the urinal trough.
> I liked it rough. From behind the stall,
> Lady Pearl slurred the words: *Don't hold out for love.*

This sounds pretty personal, doesn't it? But then, one can turn to the online magazine *La Petite Zine* and find lines like these from Matthea Harvey:

> All bright thought lay in future thought.
>
> The coin was in the puddin hid.
>
> Cod from the machine will not do,
> said the dramaturg-turned-nutritionist.

Only the upper echelons could afford to be
nonchalant about it. They were, as in, oh.

It was the first time a lost Jocelyn
& a found Jocelyn had turned out

to be not one & the same . . .

Not so personal, are they? How much of our personal
lives belong in poems is a question that has occupied the po-
etry world for a century. And it remains unsettled in part
because nobody—certainly not us poets—seems to be sure
exactly what we mean by "personal."

That may seem like a curious claim; after all, surely if
there's one thing we know, it's what makes us *us*. But con-
sider the following sentences, assuming for the moment that
all are true:

Bob Smith was born on November 9, 1971.
Bob Smith's favorite password is "nutmeg456."
Bob Smith's Social Security number is
    987-65-4320.
Bob Smith has a foot fetish.
As a child, Bob Smith had an imaginary friend named
    Mr. Pigwort.
Whenever Bob Smith hears the sound of a high wind,
    it makes him think of his wife, who died ten years

earlier, and he hears her voice faintly calling, as if from a great distance.

The first three sentences contain deeply *private* information—indeed, information that might enable someone to steal Mr. Smith's identity—but they likely don't seem personal in the way that the last three might. (And which of those last three you consider the most intimate will depend on how you look at the world.) The point here is that our conception of "the personal" has to do with more than the data of our lives, no matter how sensitive. It has to do with how we see ourselves, how we see others, how we imagine others see us, how they actually see us, and the potential embarrassment, joy, and shame that occur at the intersection of these different perspectives.

———

But why, you might wonder, do poets need to be concerned about any of this in the first place? Why do so many people who don't read much poetry (and quite a few who do) reflexively assume that poems generally relate, in however uncertain and attenuated a manner, to a writer's "real life"? Why are we amused by a comment like "You mean you criticize people's *poetry*?" rather than simply perplexed, as we would be if someone said, "You mean you criticize people's *novels*?" or "You mean you criticize people's *narrative nonfiction*?" After all, in order for a joke to be funny, we have to get the premise. Why is the premise that poetry has something to do with our inner lives something that we automatically understand? Shouldn't it be possible for us to read poems without thinking about "the personal" at all?

The short answer is: of course. Poetry has historically included many genres—the epic, the short narrative poem, the occasional poem—that have little to do with "the personal" as it's generally understood today. And indeed, contemporary poets have worked more successfully in these genres than they are sometimes given credit for. Here, for instance, is the opening of Les Murray's novel-in-verse *Fredy Neptune*, the epic tale of Fred Boettcher, an itinerant Australian mariner who witnesses much of the worst violence of the twentieth century:

> That was sausage day
> on our farm outside Dungog.
> There's my father Reinhard Boettcher,
> my mother Agnes. There is brother Frank
> who died of the brain-burn, meningitis.
> There I am having my turn
> at the mincer. Cooked meat with parsley and salt
> winding out, smooth as gruel, for the weisswurst.

The "facts" of *Fredy Neptune* don't point us in the direction of facts that might pertain to Les Murray. That isn't to claim that Les Murray's personal history has nothing to do with the poem, but only to suggest that the poem itself doesn't signal us to check its claims against any identity we might associate with Murray. It's an obvious point, to be sure, but it's nonetheless helpful to bear in mind that poetry like Murray's 250-page novel is no less poetic than the soppiest verse about a love affair gone wrong. And beyond the traditionally depersonalized narrative genres represented by work like *Fredy Neptune*, there is the extravagantly formal world of the academic avant-garde, in which poets write books that consist entirely of a transcription of a year's worth of weather reports. A sense of "the real person" tends to go by the wayside when you're looking at lines like "Mostly clear, overnight lows 40°F, Precip 0%."

But in a sense, these examples, however interesting and worth talking about, are sidestepping the question. When people talk about poetry being personal, they aren't thinking of poems about Australian seamen or about northerly winds in Boise. They're thinking about poems in which an "I" says something about itself, or the world, or a "You"—and does so in such a way that we experience something like the thrill of discovery. They are thinking, in other words, about the lyric.

———

Here it's best to clarify some terms. Billy Collins has an amusing poem about the words used most frequently in contemporary poems ("light" figures prominently); in contemporary poetry criticism, we have our own commonplace terms, and the most conspicuous of these is probably "lyric." What, exactly, is the lyric, and why do critics like to talk about it so much?

Historically speaking, this is an easy question to answer. Lyric is one of the three classical modes of poetry—the other two being narrative and dramatic—and it's traditionally considered to be closely related to song. But this antique description tells us relatively little about lyric poetry today. According to *The New Princeton Encyclopedia of Poetry and Poetics*, the modern lyric has been "employed in the causes of self-expression, feminism, and racial and social equality." But it has also apparently become "a device for making the invisible visible" in which "[t]he poet-surrogate is replaced by the figurative voice, a mantic or shamanistic presence . . ." So it's connected to "self-expression" except when it's connected to some kind of prophetic voice that has nothing to do with "the poet-surrogate." In fact, the only thing the *Princeton Encyclopedia* seems to be sure of about the lyric is that it's overwhelmingly popular.

Which seems about right. There's been a great deal of confusion over the lyric mode over the past hundred years, mostly because of the genre's extreme versatility. In the way that a stick can serve as firewood, an imaginary rifle, or a dowsing rod, the lyric has been many things to many poets, and it would be a mistake to pretend otherwise. Probably the most that can safely be said nowadays is that lyrics are short(ish) and present a unified sensibility, often involving the use of a voice calling itself "I," that may or may not represent the writer as he perceives himself. Even given that rather nebulous definition, however, the potential significance of lyricism to "the personal" seems clear: If I want to tell you something personal, then it probably makes sense if "I" am the one saying it.

For that reason, one of the more popular ways to explain the abundance of personal material in contemporary poetry is simply to say that "personalism" flows naturally from our preference for the lyric mode, as opposed to the narrative-based poem, or the verse drama, or what have you. A few years ago, I published a review in which I puzzled over the idea of "personal" writing, and a talented peer of mine, Joshua Weiner, wrote in to offer what seems a fair representation of this line of argument. Weiner said:

> In his discussion . . . David Orr wonders about "the
> personal flavor that readers desire" from poetry, a
> kind of writing that we supposedly like to think of as
> "personal." The question Orr doesn't ask directly is
> how we've come to presume that what we talk about
> when we talk about current poetry is the lyric (and
> not the epic, epistle, satire, dramatic monologue, etc.).
> It's not a flavor that draws readers, as Orr puts it—it's
> a sound, an intimate sound memorably figured. It is
> a mystery but not, as Orr also claims, a muddle. The
> sound of a single voice singing to each of us is a primal

experience of reception, connection, and transmission. The experience is part of our cognitive growth; we're probably hardwired by it.

There are several things in this passage that seem interestingly right to me (the idea that we're hardwired by our response to lyric utterance is intriguing), but there are several things that are interestingly wrong as well. Foremost among these is the suggestion that lyricism seems personal because, well, it just *is*. If you read a lot of contemporary poetry, then it's easy to feel that this is the case—there are more transparently veiled personal references in modern poems than there are grits in South Carolina. But in point of fact, lyricism isn't necessarily personal. It isn't even usually personal. Take this lyric, for example:

A-tisket, a-tasket
A green and yellow basket
I wrote a letter to my love
And on the way I dropped it

I dropped it, I dropped it
Yes, on the way I dropped it
A little girlie picked it up
And took it to the market

She was truckin' on down the avenue
Without a single thing to do

She was peck, peck, peckin' all around
When she spied it on the ground

It's hard to argue that audiences don't respond to this particular lyric—it's been covered or referenced by everyone from Ella Fitzgerald to Eminem—but it's unlikely that people have embraced it because they think the words had personal relevance for the original tisketer, whoever that was. Probably they just like the way it sounds. From Sappho to Thomas Wyatt to Cole Porter, lyrics have a long and rich history of having little or nothing to do with the private identities of their composers—and while it's true that song lyrics and modern poetic lyrics operate in very different contexts, there's nothing inherent to either mode that makes those contexts inevitable.

Moreover, even when poetic lyrics do seem personal, it's sometimes the case that the experience we're having has less to do with "the personal" as I've been discussing it here, and more to do with what might be better described as "the intimate." Intimacy in lyric poetry, as in life, is a kind of relationship: It assumes that "we" understand one another, that "we" might be able to disclose things to each other of a personal nature. But it doesn't require that we actually say those things. For instance, Philip Larkin's short lyric "Talking in Bed," like much of Larkin's work, encourages intimacy with the reader without resorting to anything that is explicitly "personal" on the poet's part:

Talking in bed ought to be easiest,
Lying together there goes back so far,
An emblem of two people being honest.

Yet more and more time passes silently.
Outside, the wind's incomplete unrest
Builds and disperses clouds about the sky,

And dark towns heap up on the horizon.
None of this cares for us. Nothing shows why
At this unique distance from isolation

It becomes still more difficult to find
Words at once true and kind,
Or not untrue and not unkind.

Notice that Larkin isn't actually telling us anything unique about himself here. Instead, he's attempting to win our assent to a generalization; to form a bond between reader and writer that allows us to sigh knowingly and say, "Yes, it *is* like that sometimes—for all of us." Naturally, we may feel that we're getting a view of the way Larkin's mind works, or the way his sensibility as a poet operates—we may think we know him, to an extent—but we aren't actually getting any information about the existence of Philip Larkin beyond his identity as the poem's author. (Indeed, the more Larkin insisted on the personal nature of his feelings, the more dif-

ficult it might be for him to get us to share them.) This is very
different from the sense we get from the opening of "Flee on
Your Donkey" by Anne Sexton:

> Because there was no other place
> to flee to,
> I came back to the scene of the disordered senses,
> came back last night at midnight,
> arriving in the thick June night
> without luggage or defenses,
> giving up my car keys and my cash,
> keeping only a pack of Salem cigarettes
> the way a child holds on to a toy.
> I signed myself in where a stranger
> puts the inked-in X's —
> for this is a mental hospital,
> not a child's game.

Larkin's and Sexton's poems are aiming for very differ-
ent things. Larkin wants us to consent to a shared identity;
Sexton wants us to acknowledge the uniqueness of her own.

———

But now it seems reasonable to ask: What exactly *is* the "per-
sonal"? So far we've mostly looked at what it isn't: It's not
raw fact data like Social Security numbers, it's not lyricism,
it's not even lyric intimacy. Nor is "the personal" quite the

same as the large-scale sensibility that we come to identify with certain highly accomplished writers; the quality, for instance, that makes Elizabeth Bishop's poetry feel like *Bishop*, or John Ashbery's feel like *Ashbery*. There's something personal about an accomplishment of that nature, certainly, but the perfected identity of a major artist is very different from "the personal" as one generally experiences it. Usually "the personal" seems less solid and more vulnerable; less poised and more precarious. Often it feels on the brink of being, well, embarrassing.

That sense of embarrassment is, in fact, one of the keys to understanding what we're talking about when we talk about "personal" poetry. Think about the remark with which this chapter began: "You mean you criticize people's *poetry?*" Implicit in this question is the assumption that poetry involves a kind of vulnerability, and that taking advantage of this vulnerability (in order to make a clever criticism, for example) is somehow cruel. Cruel, one might say, because it could lead to embarrassment. Indeed, the possibility of embarrassment hovers over personal writing like the possibility of bad weather hovers over ships at sea: It charges each moment with the risk of destabilization, and gives each successfully executed maneuver an electric, wave-topping flair. But the embarrassment we associate with the personal is a very particular and peculiar phenomenon. It's only loosely related, for example, to the embarrassment we feel when confronted with displays of simple incompetence. For instance, consider the last stanza of William McGonagall's legendarily dreadful "The Tay Bridge Disaster," which is possibly the worst poem ever written about a public calamity:

> It must have been an awful sight,
> To witness in the dusky moonlight,
> While the Storm Fiend did laugh, and angry did bray,
> Along the Railway Bridge of the Silv'ry Tay,
> Oh! ill-fated Bridge of the Silv'ry Tay,
> I must now conclude my lay
> By telling the world fearlessly without the least
>   dismay,
> That your central girders would not have given way,
> At least many sensible men do say,
> Had they been supported on each side with
>   buttresses,
> At least many sensible men confesses,
> For the stronger we our houses do build,
> The less chance we have of being killed.

This is embarrassing, no question, but it probably doesn't strike you as being personal. But now consider "Saved from Myself" by the pop singer Jewel, which appears in her collection *A Night Without Armor*, the best-selling debut volume of poetry ever published by an American:

How often I've cried out
in silent tongue
to be saved
from myself

in the middle of the night
too afraid
to move

horrified the answer
may be beyond the
capability of my
own two hands
so small

(no one should feel this alone)

Like McGonagall's poem, "Saved from Myself" is badly
written (grandiose phrases like "in silent tongue" are the
calling cards of the amateur poet; they practically announce
that A Poem Is Happening). So Jewel's poem, again like
McGonagall's, is embarrassing in the sense that it's clumsy.
But it may also strike you as being somehow "personally"
embarrassing—or at any rate, more personally embarrass-
ing than "The Tay Bridge Disaster." Why is that the case?

One obvious answer would be to say that Jewel is talk-
ing about herself, whereas McGonagall is talking about

a bridge collapse. There's some truth to that, but it hurries past several important objections. After all, how do we know Jewel is talking about herself? Couldn't she be using the "figurative voice" that the *Princeton Encyclopedia* mentions? And even assuming that she is talking about herself, why would that necessarily make the poem "personally" embarrassing? The basic sentiment she's expressing—*I am imprisoned within my own consciousness, woe is me, etc.*—isn't all that different from the one conveyed in Frost's "Acquainted with the Night" or Eliot's "The Waste Land" or Matthew Arnold's "Dover Beach" or any number of other well-regarded poems by well-regarded poets.

To understand what makes Jewel's poem seem so personal, not to mention so unfortunate, it helps to imagine the following situation: You're in a karaoke bar listening to two singers perform back-to-back. Both are fully committed to performing their songs well. The first singer has picked a relatively innocuous tune by Jimmy Buffett about getting drunk in the Caribbean. He proceeds to mangle the chorus and sing the entire song in the wrong key. The second singer has chosen the ballad "My Heart Will Go On" from the movie *Titanic* and prefaces the song by announcing that the performance is dedicated "to my mother, who died of cancer last month." As he lifts the microphone, you notice that a tear is wandering down his cheek, and that his hands are shaking a little, possibly from nervousness. He opens his mouth, takes a breath, and pours forth with complete sincerity the sound of an abused kazoo.

My guess is that while you'd feel embarrassed for both singers, you'd have an especially wincing, sympathetic reaction to the second, just as you might feel a protective embarrassment on Jewel's behalf that you don't feel for McGonagall. And you'd feel that way, at least in part, because the singer had brought together two things that don't fit naturally together: performing in a karaoke bar and grieving for a loved one. That's not to say those two activities could never be combined successfully, but any such combination would require considerable finesse on the part of the performer and flexibility on the part of the audience. This is a challenge faced by "personal" poets as well, because their poems are always a kind of performance in which the poet-as-author/ performer must be reconciled with the poet-as-he-appears-in-the-poem. As it happens, this challenge is in keeping with the basic mechanisms of embarrassment as described by the sociologist Erving Goffman, whose theories about why and how we become embarrassed have been influential in several fields over the past half century. As Goffman puts it in *Interaction Rituals*,

> [o]ften important everyday occasions of
> embarrassment arise when the self projected is
> somehow confronted with another self which, though
> valid in other contexts, cannot be here sustained in

harmony with the first. Embarrassment, then, leads us
to the matter of "role segregation."

Admittedly, we should always be careful when using
one discipline's terms to describe phenomena in different
arenas. Still, it seems fair to say that when a poem seems
personal to us, the experience we're having relates closely
to Goffman's idea of "role segregation," in the sense that an
identity we view as more "private" seems to be entering the
poem. We have trouble keeping the poet-as-author "sus-
tained in harmony" with this new identity (or identities, as
the case may be), in part because the writer himself seems
to struggle to do so. In Jewel's "Saved from Myself," for
instance, we might call this other presence something like
Jewel-in-extremis, or maybe just Jewel-as-she-sniffles-
into-her-pillow-after-a-bad-day. Whatever we call it, it
supplies us with another, obviously less public "version" of
Jewel, and the friction between this version and the version
of Jewel-as-poet can be exciting. Or as it happens, embar-
rassing.

———

It may seem as if this is little more than an elaborate way of
saying that in "personal" poetry, the "I" in the poem seems
inseparable from the author himself, the same person who
walks around, gets coffee, eats cheeseburgers, and pulls for
the Steelers. That's not the case, however, and while the

distinctions here may be subtle, they're essential to understanding how we experience "the personal." As I mentioned earlier, the information we view as personal in poems doesn't usually come from the raw data of our lives—bar tabs and tax filings and such—but rather from the murky and constantly shifting intersections among private identities and public observance. Consequently, our view of "the personal" depends less on content than on context: What seems personal depends upon where (and how) it's said. Because we are different things to different people at different times, it's more helpful to think about combining unlike identities than it is to talk about "the 'I' of the poem" and "the author himself" (who is better thought of as a combination of selves, some of them potentially more personal in particular moments than others). Or to put it another way: What we experience as personal isn't a matter of revelation, but a question of juxtaposition.

Consider the case of Frank O'Hara. Perhaps no twentieth-century American writer is more commonly associated with the concept of personal presence; certainly few American poets are anywhere near as personable. O'Hara is famous for what are often called "I do this, I do that" poems, in which the "I" of the poem is closely attached to the writer-as-physical-person through near-constant observations about facts, times, places, and people—which is a long-winded way of saying that O'Hara writes in a seemingly casual way about what he's doing and looking at. Here's the beginning of "A Step Away from Them":

It's my lunch hour, so I go
for a walk among the hum-colored
cabs. First, down the sidewalk
where laborers feed their dirty
glistening torsos sandwiches
and Coca-Cola, with yellow helmets
on. They protect them from falling
bricks, I guess. Then onto the
avenue where skirts are flipping
above heels and blow up over
grates. The sun is hot, but the
cabs stir up the air. I look
at bargains in wristwatches. There
are cats playing in sawdust . . .

As you can see, O'Hara isn't interested in carefully calculated artistic distance; he's interested in an equally calculated artistic presence.

But how personal does that presence really seem? Not very, I'd say. And O'Hara relies on that in order to give us an abrupt contrast later in the poem; note the sections that I've bolded:

. . . There are several Puerto
Ricans on the avenue today, which
makes it beautiful and warm. **First
Bunny died, then John Latouche,
then Jackson Pollock. But is the**

earth as full as life was full, of them?
And one has eaten and one walks,
past the magazines with nudes
and the posters for BULLFIGHT and
the Manhattan Storage Warehouse,
which they'll soon tear down. I
used to think they had the Armory
Show there.
    A glass of papaya juice
and back to work. **My heart is in my**
pocket, it is Poems by Pierre Reverdy.

This tactic of piling up prosaic details, and then shifting rapidly into another register is one of O'Hara's signature maneuvers. He uses it again in his much-anthologized elegy for Billie Holiday "The Day Lady Died," which opens, "It is 12:20 in New York a Friday / three days after Bastille Day, yes / it is 1959, and I go get a shoeshine / because I will get off the 4:19 in East Hampton / at 7:15 . . ." The "I" here is surely the Frank O'Hara who walks around and gets coffee. But the poem ends:

 . . . I go back where I came from to 6th Avenue
 and the tobacconist in the Ziegfeld Theatre and
 casually ask for a carton of Gauloises and a carton
 of Picayunes, and a NEW YORK POST with her face on it
 and I am sweating a lot by now and thinking of
 leaning on the john door in the 5 SPOT

while she whispered a song along the keyboard
to Mal Waldron and everyone and I stopped breathing.

What do we make of these bolded sections? As you can see, they're different from the other lines in tone, mood, and often diction. They almost seem to belong to a different poem.

Or perhaps simply to another identity. One of O'Hara's great virtues is his delicately nuanced understanding of embarrassment, of what will make us feel that a rock has broken the stillness of the social order, however quickly and quietly that order may be restored. In poems like "The Day Lady Died," O'Hara relies upon our sense that some experiences—grief, for example—actually *don't* sit very easily alongside our day-to-day activities, so that when they're brought up abruptly in a poem filled with ephemera, we're forced to decide whether the sudden emergence of this other, more personal identity can be accommodated. It's a risky strategy, because it requires a pitch-perfect sense of decorum. Just consider, for instance, how you'd respond if "The Day Lady Died" ended like this:

. . . I go back where I came from to 6th Avenue
and the tobacconist in the Ziegfeld Theatre and
casually ask for a carton of Gauloises and a carton
of Picayunes, and a NEW YORK POST with her face on it
and I am sweating a lot by now and thinking about
how I'll never hear her voice again, the voice

that made me feel so alive, so special,
that the loss of it is . . . AAAARRRGHHH! I can't
    breathe!
No one should feel this alone.

Not quite so good, is it? Like the karaoke singer who mourns his mother, O'Hara is attempting to reconcile disparate identities; unlike the karaoke singer, he has the skill to pull it off. But we experience "The Day Lady Died" as personal not because we've seen "the real Frank O'Hara," but because we've seen a different, more private O'Hara beside the one who visits the tobacconist in the Ziegfeld Theatre, and set against the O'Hara who has written the poem.

———

The personal, then, is always relative. This is an easy truth to lose track of, however, because certain information seems so obviously personal that it's hard to imagine not reading it as such. Surely, we think, the secrets of our relationships must be personal, along with our memories of our families, our doubts about ourselves, our secret, quiet struggles with various compulsions and obsessions, our love for the stuffed hippo we got when we were five, and which is now missing one of its glossy green plastic eyes, which always reminded us of those summer days, when Mom and Dad would take us to the park, and we would all . . . Well. In any case, the idea that certain facts can reliably guide us to "the personal" can be hard to resist.

Indeed, that idea lies at the center of the poetic practice known as confessionalism, which for about half a century has been the type of poetry most often identified with "the personal"—in this case, a personal sense dependent on the announcement of private facts that might be embarrassing, disturbing, or simply the kind of thing usually considered indiscreet. Confessionalism was given its Official Literary Christening in a 1959 review of Robert Lowell's *Life Studies* by the critic M. L. Rosenthal. Lowell, Rosenthal wrote,

> . . . removes the mask. His speaker is unequivocally himself, and it is hard not to think of *Life Studies* as a series of personal confidences, rather shameful, that one is honor-bound not to reveal. About half the book . . . is essentially a public discrediting of his father's manliness and character, as well as of the family and social milieu of his childhood. Another section . . . reinforces and even repeats these motifs, bringing them to bear on the poet's psychological problems as an adult.

Anyone who's watched daytime television will recognize the issues here. Around the same time that Lowell was skewering his father, Sylvia Plath was taking shots at her mother, husband, and just about everybody else; W. D. Snodgrass was talking through his early divorce; and Sexton was giving readers notes on her mental health and sex life. The extreme disclosure that we associate with confessionalism circa 1960 seemed shocking to many at the time, and is therefore sometimes spoken of as if it were a new development in lyric poetry. As many critics have noted, however, it can be traced back at least as far as Catullus, who wrote plenty of bitingly self-descriptive passages circa 50 B.C., as Peter Green's translation of Catullus 76 demonstrates:

> O gods, if it's in you to pity, or if you've ever rendered
>   help at the last to those on the verge of death,
> look down on my misery, and if I've lived life cleanly,
>   pluck out of me this destruction, this plague,
> which, creeping torpor-like into my inmost being
>   has emptied my heart of joy.
> I no longer ask that she return my love, or—
>   an impossibility—agree to be chaste.
> What I long for is health, to cast off this unclean sickness.

So what we're talking about when we say "confessional" is a very old tendency in lyric poetry that happens to have achieved unusual prominence over the last half century. The premise of this sort of writing is straightforward: As Rosenthal suggests, it asks us to assume that the facts related by the "I" of the poem are in basic concordance with the facts relating to the poet-as-he-walks-around.

But as we've seen, this is a tricky business, because the personal depends upon juxtapositions, not revelations. Even though Rosenthal says that Lowell "removes the mask," it would be more accurate to say that Lowell is adding new decorations to his previous mask—and while these decorations may distract us temporarily, they're unlikely to provide that personal frisson over the long term. This is the case for two reasons. First, identities are shaped in many ways in poems, only one of which is the citation of autobiographical facts, however extreme. Depending on the situation, declaring, "My father drank himself to death" may be less helpful in creating the sensation of identity than writing something like "Cold dark deep and absolutely clear, the clear gray icy water . . ." The second reason, which is related to the first, is that as more and more autobiographical references are used to anchor a poem, those facts become increasingly like any other set of external facts: They cease to surprise us on their own, and instead become the context in which surprises can happen.

Which is to say, we get used to them. Even the most aggressively disclosing sensibility can become—not old, necessarily, but anticipatable. Consider, for instance, "Sunday Night" by Sharon Olds, from her 2002 collection, *The Unswept Room*:

When the family would go to a restaurant,
my father would put his hand up a waitress's
skirt if he could—hand, wrist,

forearm. Suddenly, you couldn't see
his elbow, just the upper arm.
His teeth were wet, the whites of his eyes
wet, a man with the stump of an arm . . .

This is disturbing and seemingly personal, no doubt. But
it appears within ten pages of this:

Somehow I never stopped to notice
that my father liked to dress as a woman.
He had his sign language about women
talking too much, and being stupid,
but whenever there was a costume party
he would dress like us, the tennis balls
for breasts—balls for breasts—the pageboy
blond wig, the lipstick, he would sway
his body with moves of gracefulness . . .

Which is not too far from this:

. . . the harm my father
did us is receding. I never thought
it would happen, I thought his harm was stronger than
    that,
like God's harm—flood, or birth without
eyes, with mounds of tissue, no retina, no
pupil, the way my father on the couch did not

seem not to be using eyes,
but not to have them, or to have objects
for eyes . . .

Which picks up the thread from Olds's previous book:

I saw my father naked, once, I
opened the blue bathroom door
which he always locked—if it opened, it was empty—
and there, surrounded by glistening turquoise
tile, sitting on the toilet, was my father,
all of him, and all of him
was skin.

And we could go on. As you can see, this kind of thing
lacks the curious juxtaposition that O'Hara manages, and
it's much more controlled than Jewel's "Saved from Myself."
Consequently, we don't feel that we're being asked to rec-
oncile different identities in Olds's poetry; rather, it seems
that we're getting a remarkably consistent identity that just
happens to be extremely interested in its family travails. This
doesn't mean that Olds writes poorly, it just means that her
work doesn't necessarily read as personal even though it in-
volves indisputably "personal" material. The more we see of
her father and his various deficiencies, the more they seem
to inhabit the same role that, as Larkin once joked, daffodils
played for Wordsworth.

So one way to explain why poems filled with seemingly personal information don't automatically have a personal effect would be to say that their disclosures can quickly become conventions. The information may still be artfully deployed, and the risk involved is still substantial—but that risk is the normal risk of technical failure, not the peculiar risk of personal embarrassment.

It's helpful here to underscore something that you may already have gathered: What we view as "personal" is often in tension with what we view as "skillful" or "accomplished." That's because the "personal" typically involves what appears to be either an actual loss of control on the poet's part (as with Jewel) or a teetering-on-the-brink (as with O'Hara), and both scenarios run counter to our usual ideas about skill. Indeed, strong personal poems like "The Day Lady Died" make the distinction between words like "artful" and "artless" so complicated as to be almost impenetrable. If we view the poem as artful, we ignore the extent to which our response to it depends on the lines *not* seeming "thought out," "crafted," "manipulated"—the adjectives we associate with skill and mastery. If we view the poem as somehow artless, though, we ignore the extent to which its success is plainly the result (at least in part) of the poet's deliberate decision-making, rather than his sincerity or good intentions or luck. Good "personal" poems, then, almost always have a slightly improvised feel— like magic tricks composed on the spot. Again, it helps to think of these distinctions in terms of embarrassment: A person can rescue himself from a situation that might inspire our sympathetic embarrassment, but if he plans the situation in advance—and we know it—our embarrassed response probably won't be triggered. The "personal" poet, then, is in the odd position of scripting an improvisation (and we'll set aside the extremely complicated question of when a poetic performance occurs).

This tension between technical achievement and "the personal" has been a twentieth- and twenty-first century preoccupation, but earlier poets have struggled with the same concern. In fact, one of the best examinations of these issues appears in Robert Browning's "One Word More" from 1855, which focuses on the attraction artists sometimes feel for art forms other than their own. "Of all the artists living, loving," Browning tells us,

> None but would forego his proper dowry,
> Does he paint? he fain would write a poem,
> Does he write? he fain would paint a picture,

And each artist has this wish to participate in a different art form, according to Browning, because

> . . . Heaven's gift takes earth's abatement!
> He who smites the rock and spreads the water,
> Bidding drink and live a crowd beneath him,

Even he, the minute makes immortal,
Proves, perchance, but mortal in the minute.
Desecrates, belike, the deed in doing.

In other words, like Moses, the poet is always in the posi-
tion of performing the miraculous (or at any rate, the clever
and interesting); but because he knows how to do so, and has
done so before, "the doing savors of disrelish." As a result,
he finds himself wanting to say something that exists beyond
his proven gift for saying things. He wants to create art that
isn't art. He wants to be, one might say, personal.

This helps explain why the general reader often views
modern poetry as more personal even than memoir. Sure,
the memoirist, like the confessional poet, is telling us deep
and ugly things about himself—but we've seen this trick be-
fore. We know how the water rises from this particular rock;
we know that it will always taste faintly of iron, as from
having passed over underground machinery set in familiar
motion. Poetry, though, remains largely unknown to many
readers, and therefore better able to surprise us with its dis-
tinctive miracles. Think of it this way: If you were listening
to a paid performance by a trained singer of an especially
moving song, you probably wouldn't think, "I'm gaining a
glimpse of something *personal* about this performer!" Any-
one who goes to a Beyoncé concert and afterward thinks that
he "knows" Beyoncé is in line for a temporary restraining
order. But imagine how you might feel if you came unan-
nounced to a friend's house and overheard him giving an

impassioned version of, say, "One" by U2. You *would* think you'd learned something about your friend. You might feel embarrassed for him. And the reason for both responses, at least in part, would be that you'd feel that you had heard something you weren't supposed to hear; that your friend had been in an obscure way caught out. You had seen an identity you weren't supposed to see.

This is how many readers think of poetry. Such readers don't imagine poetry to be something they hear, they consider it something that is, as John Stuart Mill once claimed, "overheard"—and this belief is a function, at least in part, of how unfamiliar readers are with what constitutes poetic practice. We understand the context in which memoirists work, we appreciate that while such writers are indeed telling us secrets, they are also "putting on a show" for us that we're entitled to find good, bad, boring, or electrifying. We're not so sure about poets. That uncertainty can make it difficult for us to tell when something "personal" is happening in a poem; it can also cause us to confuse imitations of private information with the real thing (as when poets write poems involving sisters they don't have, or houses they've never lived in). Consider Frederick Seidel's "That Fall":

> The body on the bed is made of china,
> Shiny china vagina and pubic hair.
> The glassy smoothness of a woman's body!
> I stand outside the open door and stare.

I watch the shark glide by . . . it comes and goes—
Must constantly keep moving or it will drown.
The mouth slit in the formless fetal nose
Gives it that empty look—it looks unborn;

It comes into the room up to the bed
Just like a dog. The smell of burning leaves,
Rose bittersweetness rising from the red,
Is what I see. I must be twelve. That fall.

Is this "personal"? Is it "a true story"? I'd say the former
and not necessarily the latter—but part of that judgment in-
volves knowing that Seidel is writing both out of and against
the poetry of private fact as practiced by Robert Lowell.
Part of it also involves being familiar with the way in which
poets can use differences in register—for example, the Pre-
Raphaelite smoothness of "Rose bittersweetness rising from
the red" as opposed to the deliberate clumsiness of "shiny
china vagina"—to create the kind of tension we associate
with "the personal." And of course, part of that judgment
simply comes from having read a good bit of Seidel's writing.

———

But if audiences aren't always sure what to do with poetry,
poets are often equally uncertain about what to do with au-
diences. In his study *The Idea of Lyric*, W. R. Johnson talks
about the way in which (as he sees it) the modern poetic lyric
has moved from an "I" speaking to a "You" to an "I" speak-

ing to itself or to nothing. Is it any surprise that an art form whose conventions are largely unknown, and whose practitioners often seem to be addressing themselves, has come to be seen—by lay readers, anyway—as presumptively personal? As something it seems cruel to criticize? Probably not. But it's worth thinking about how much richer those readers' experience might be if they had a slightly greater acquaintance with the many ways in which poetry can be impersonal; at the least, this would help explain the strange ways in which it actually *can* be personal. In a small, unfashionable, and very fine poem called "Country Stars," William Meredith advises us to "have no fear, or only proper fear" of the natural world, because no matter what we do, "the bright watchers"—that is, the stars—"are still there." It would be a good thing for readers to have no embarrassment, or only proper embarrassment, when reading poems, if only so that they could get a clearer glimpse of the poets behind them. Who will still be there, regardless.

the political

SHORTLY BEFORE THE 2008 Democratic primary in Ohio, Tom Buffenbarger, the head of the machinists' union and a supporter of Hillary Clinton, took to the stage at a Clinton rally in Youngstown to lay the wood to Barack Obama. "Give me a break," snarled Buffenbarger, "I've got news for all the latte-drinking, Prius-driving, Birkenstock-wearing, trust fund babies crowding in to hear him speak! This guy won't last a round against the Republican attack machine." And then the union rep delivered his coup de grace: "He's a poet, not a fighter!"

Ouch.

Fortunately, this insult to the sacred mysteries of Poesie didn't go unanswered—within a few days, the poet John Lundberg angrily riposted at the Huffington Post, declaring that he "would be happy to step outside" with Buffenbarger to show him that poets can indeed mix it up. Yet what was most interesting about the Clinton supporter's remarks wasn't their inaccuracy or intemperance, but the way in which they neatly summarized two assumptions often made about contemporary American poetry and contemporary American politics. Loosely speaking, these are:

1. That poetry is passive, swoony, and generally not in the business of "doing things."
2. That politics is active, gritty, and comparable to war.

Many objections can be made to these assumptions, but it's important to note first that poetry and politics are both matters of verbal persuasion—that is, both have strong connections to the old art of rhetoric. Admittedly, poets and politicians are typically trying to persuade us of very different things, yet the two worlds have far more in common with each other than either does with, for instance, the world of Brazilian jujitsu. In light of that, one would think poets might get a little more respect from political speakers, and that political speakers might refrain from comparing their purely verbal existence to the decidedly nonverbal world of physical violence.

But they don't. Instead, the relationship between American poetry and American politics is confused and confusing, with politicians sometimes describing the highest moments in political life as "poetic" ("I have a dream . . .")

and other times offering up poetry as a symbol of empty talk. And of course, American poets are even more conflicted. Rare is the poet who doesn't view himself as deeply invested in political life, and yet the sloppy, compromised, and frequently idiotic business of democracy—which is, for all its flaws, the way most political change occurs in this country—rarely attracts the attention of our best poets. Is this the inevitable order of things? Or are all the talkers simply talking past each other?

———

That question is especially important for poets, because they do a lot—a lot a lot a lot—of talking about how poetry fits into the political world. Possibly it isn't immediately obvious to you that poets and the various choices they make are essential elements in our democracy. Possibly you think that the average voter, upon being told that a group of poets felt strongly about a particular issue, would be less likely to say, "Well, then I am persuaded!" than to say, "We have poets? Do they wear capes?" Possibly you doubt that it really matters, politicswise, whether somebody gets a poem published in a magazine with a circulation in the low hundreds, or writes a long post exposing the evils of the Academy of American Poets on a blog called The Dread Schenectady.

This is why you are not a poet, or at least not a particular kind of poet. For hark at the talk that goes on in Poetryland:

I think that disjunctive and non-sequential writing can change states of consciousness, awakening the reader to reality, and thus the need for political change.

—HANNAH WEINER, POET, IN *The Politics of Poetic Form: Poetry and Public Policy*

Through men like Dana Gioia, John Barr, and Ted Kooser [three poets whom the author associates with the Poetry Foundation], Karl Rove's battle-tested blend of unapologetic economic elitism and reactionary cultural populism is now being marketed in the far-off reaches of the poetry world.

—STEPHEN EVANS, PROFESSOR AT THE UNIVERSITY OF MAINE

If the Bush people thought canceling the poetry symposium would quell the rising tide of voices joining Poets Against the War, they must have been shocked, if not awed, by the response.

—SAM HAMILL, FORMER EDITOR OF COPPER CANYON PRESS

Is it facile to connect the fortunes of American poetry in the largest sense with the partisan nature of the federal government? Maybe, maybe not . . .

—DAVID LEHMAN, EDITOR OF THE BEST AMERICAN POETRY SERIES

It may seem odd that an art form so determinedly ignored by most Americans spends this much energy talking about its role in the political life of those very same Americans. (Lest it seem that I'm singling out leftist poets in the above quotations, I should add that almost all poets, including myself, lean left. There are maybe five conservative American poets, not one of whom can safely show his face at a writing conference for fear of being angrily doused with herbal tea.) We don't spend much time wondering what poetry has to do with neuroscience or television writing or college basketball, yet these are important areas of American existence that involve assertions about truth, form, morality, and the nature of culture—all subjects regularly claimed as poetry's turf. Yet the connection between poetry and politics interests the poetry world in ways that the arguably more obvious connection between poetry and linguistics does not. Why?

The ideal answer to that question would involve a painstaking analysis of the political inclinations of several hundred years' worth of English language poets, and it would take a proper scholar at least two books to outline. That answer would also be dull, so let's instead consider two quotes, one famous, one slightly less so. The first is from Percy Bysshe Shelley in 1821:

The most unfailing herald, companion, and follower
of the awakening of a great people to work a beneficial
change in opinion or institution, is poetry . . . [Poets]

measure the circumference and sound the depths
of human nature with a comprehensive and all-
penetrating spirit, and they are themselves perhaps the
most sincerely astonished at its manifestations; for it
is less their spirit than the spirit of the age. Poets are
the hierophants of an unapprehended inspiration; the
mirrors of the gigantic shadows which futurity casts
upon the present; the words which express what they
understand not; the trumpets which sing to battle,
and feel not what they inspire; the influence which is
moved not, but moves. Poets are the unacknowledged
legislators of the world.

And the second quote is from W. H. Auden in 1948:

All poets adore explosions, thunderstorms, tornadoes,
conflagrations, ruins, scenes of spectacular carnage.
The poetic imagination is not at all a desirable quality
in a statesman. In a war or revolution, a poet may
do very well as a guerrilla fighter or a spy, but it is
unlikely that he will make a good regular soldier, or, in
peace time, a conscientious member of a parliamentary
committee.

Although Auden is a levelheaded writer who's usually in
the business of undercutting people like Shelley, it's interest-
ing to notice the ways in which these very different state-

ments are based upon similar assumptions. Poets, Shelley tells us, are "the mirrors of the gigantic shadows which futurity casts upon the present"—in other words, they aren't just people who think of ways to write new poems, but people who imagine new ways of being and perceiving. It might at first be hard to see how Auden's wry description of "the poetic imagination" as a jumble of thunderstorms and explosions matches up with this conception. Yet Auden's gentle mockery begins from the premise that poetic thinking is essentially apocalyptic; that poetry involves a kind of totalizing vision to which everything, even the poet himself, becomes subordinate. Shelley thinks this vision is to be trusted; Auden thinks it should be resisted. But both believe that this is how poetry works.

It's also how democratic politics is sometimes thought to work, at least when we're thinking of politics in its more abstract incarnations. Here, for instance, is how Franklin D. Roosevelt viewed the job to which he devoted much of his life:

> The Presidency is not merely an administrative office. That's the least of it. It is more than an engineering job, efficient or inefficient. It is predominantly a place of moral leadership. All our great presidents were leaders of thought at times when certain historic ideas in the life of the nation had to be clarified.

To say that you're personally necessary in order for "certain historic ideas in the life of the nation . . . to be clarified" is only a few hyperventilating breaths short of calling yourself "a mirror of the gigantic shadow which futurity casts upon the present." The link again is the concept of totalizing vision. And this concept—dramatic, romantic, wildly generalizing—is one that politics and poetry don't share to the same degree with activities like neuroscience (which focuses on particulars) or television writing (which tends to emphasize craft). Indeed, the only other areas of American life that have similar inclinations are probably religion and philosophy. Religion is no longer attractive for many poets for reasons that are historical and beyond the scope of this chapter. Philosophizing remains a popular endeavor in the poetry world, but only so long as it's a poetic sort of philosophizing (Nietzsche, Heidegger) and not complicated, logic-y stuff that involves formulations like

$xFx \rightarrow \exists x \Diamond Fx$. Since Anglo-American philosophy has been dominated by the latter sort of thinking for decades, it's no surprise most poets don't go in for it.

Which leaves politics as the most favorable nonartistic arena for a certain type of poetic sensibility. In his essay "Absolute Poetry and Absolute Politics," the British critic Michael Hamburger argues that this sensibility, which he connects with the Romantic-Symbolist tradition, "presuppose[s] a high degree of isolation or alienation from society." Hamburger believes that poets who work in this vein have "a private religion, a *religio poetae* that is incom-

patible with the public world," and that such writers conse-
quently are attracted to "absolute political creeds, mistaking
their monomania for a dedication akin to [the poets'] own,
and seduced by promises of order." It's an interesting point,
but we can be satisfied with a more modest related argu-
ment: Any brand of politics—"absolute" or not—has a vi-
sion that supports and sustains it, and in which some poets
may find reflections of the structure they seek in their writ-
ing. Even a responsible American citizen-poet has a flicker
of the old Romantic-Symbolist fire in his belly, and this may
cause him to feel a connection to contemporary politics that
is often no less intense than Ezra Pound's affection for Il
Duce. When a contemporary poet like Jorie Graham takes
on global warming—as she does in her 2008 book, *Sea
Change*—that's more or less what's going on.

———

That connection is both enhanced and complicated by the
persistence of the lyric as contemporary poetry's dominant
mode. The modern lyric may be fractured, tweaked, or
warped, but essentially it remains a self-enclosed world cre-
ated by a singular voice (which isn't always the same thing
as a single subject called "I"). That voice is often speaking
to itself in meditative solitude, yet even as the lyric insists on
privacy, the act of insisting necessarily implies that there's
someone to be insisted *to*. This puts the lyric in a potentially
awkward position relative to the larger political world, which
is generally not paying it much attention. For American

poets, the central dilemma of the modern lyric is therefore remarkably similar to the dilemma that's often described as central to America itself: the question of individualism. As Tocqueville tells us, "Thus not only does democracy make every man forget his ancestors, but it hides his descendants and separates his contemporaries from him; it throws him back forever upon himself alone and threatens in the end to confine him entirely within the solitude of his own heart." That solitude can be poignant. Consider the beginnings of three recent books, picked more or less at random:

Toward evening, the natural light becomes
Intelligent and answers, without demur:
"Be assured! You are not alone . . ."
—FROM *Descartes' Loneliness* BY ALLEN GROSSMAN

Dress of dreams and portents, worn

in memory, despite
the posted warnings
sunk deeply into the damp
sand
all along the shore. *(The green*

tragedy of the sea
about to happen to me.)
—FROM *Lilies Without* BY LAURA KASISCHKE

I don't know what kind of man I am.

I know it was not hate I felt;
It was not the disgust and the stone in my belly.

—FROM *Rift* BY FORREST HAMER

Yet just as America has (mostly) avoided the trap Tocqueville feared, American poets find ways to reach outside themselves, however tentatively. Yes, there's a great deal of loneliness in the quotes above, but there's beauty too, and much of that beauty stems from ambivalence and ambiguity: an uncertainty about what might be said, whom it might be said to, and how it might be taken. And ambivalence isn't refusal or rejection. If poets are unsure whom to address—and by extension, unsure of their relationship with society—the modern lyric still wants to address *someone*. As a result, our poets edge toward politics, they edge away from it; but either way, they are conscious of an existence outside themselves. The path to a richer political poetry is still open.

———

And that, of course, brings us to Ralph Nader. Or rather, it brings us to the difficult question of the contemporary political poem, one of the most striking recent examples of which was posted by Ralph Nader on his website in late March 2008. Here is "Don't Listen to Senator Leahy":

Senator Clinton:

Just read where Senator Patrick

Leahy is calling on you to drop

out of the Presidential race.

Believe me.

I know something about this.

Here's my advice:

Don't listen to people when they tell you not to run

    anymore.

That's just political bigotry.

Listen to your own inner citizen First Amendment

    voice.

This is America.

Just like every other citizen, you have a right to run.

Whenever you like.

For as long as you like.

It's up to you, Hillary.

Just tell them—

It's democracy.

Get used to it.

Okay, so it's not a *good* poem. But Nader's effort, however clunky, helps to underscore the confusion we feel over "political poetry" in general. Is a political poem simply a poem with "political" words in it, like "Congress" or "Dachau" or "egalitarianism"? Or is it a poem that discusses the way people relate (or might relate) to one another? If that's the case, are love poems political? What about poems in dialect? Should we draw a firm line, and say that a political poem has to have some actual political effect? Should it attempt to persuade us in the way most normal political speech does?

Nader's poem is helpful here, because it's about as decisively political as anyone could ask. It's concerned with a specific political situation; rooted in an identifiable political philosophy; addressing a particular political actor; written in language that can be understood and appreciated by its intended audience; and finally, offered in a public forum where it can have maximum persuasive effect. More than anything else, though, "Don't Listen to Senator Leahy" is noteworthy because it's comfortable with the idea of politics as politics; it doesn't presume to stand outside the details of political life while offering judgment on that life. If the poem lacks the elegance of Tennyson's poetic advice to Gladstone on the Franchise Bill ("Steersman, be not precipitate in thine act"), it at least demonstrates a similar spirit of public involvement. There's no question that Nader knows whom he's addressing in this poem, or that he feels he has the right to do so in public.

The more typical contemporary American political poem, however, is a bit different. Consider "Bush's War" by Robert Hass:

> I typed the brief phrase, "Bush's War,"
> At the top of a sheet of white paper,
> Having some dim intuition of a poem

Made luminous by reason that would,
Though I was not sure of them entirely,
Set the facts out in an orderly way.
Berlin is a northerly city. In May
At the end of the twentieth century
In the leafy precincts of Dahlem-Dorf,
South of the Grunewald, near Krumme Lanke,
The northern spring begins before dawn
In a racket of birdsong . . .

Hass goes on to discuss the flora and fauna of the German spring, with a particular focus on asparagus, which is "served on heaped white platters / With boiled potatoes and parsley butter, / Or shavings of Parma ham and lemon juice / Or sprigs of sorrel and smoked salmon." Then he talks about wartime deaths throughout the twentieth century ("Firebombing of Tokyo, a hundred thousand / In a night"). He concludes that the real problem in the world is "a taste for power / That amounts to contempt for the body . . . It's hard to say which is worse, the moral / Sloth of it or the intellectual disgrace."

For whom is this poem intended? What is it hoping to achieve? And how can we get our hands on some of that asparagus? Hass is a greatly gifted writer with a usually reliable sense of tone, yet here, unlike Nader, he seems to be talking mostly to himself. That is, of course, always a difficult way to start a political conversation—and despite the boldly specific title, "Bush's War" turns out to have less to do with the American invasion of Iraq than with a kind of generalized horror at violence. (Otherwise, it's hard to understand what Tokyo's doing in there, aside from serving as another crudité on the atrocity platter.) In this sense, "Bush's War" is representative of a certain sort of American poem that is probably best described as "pseudo-political," because such poems fail to address their putatively political subjects in ways that recognize the practical reality of politics. They put forward no argument, make no revelatory comparison, confront no new audience, engage no misconception in language likely to be understood by the deceived, and so on and so on. Instead, they enact a version of the contemporary meditative lyric—"here I sit, having some poetic thoughts"—with a few political words taking the place of, for instance, references to waterfalls and foliage. Why do obviously politically engaged writers end up writing poems of this kind? Because it's extremely difficult for all of us (writers, plumbers, kindergarten teachers) to address people whose lives connect with our own only at obscure tangents. This is why even a poet of Hass's caliber can find himself reaching for the reassuring dialect of the university lounge, in which phrases like "moral sloth" and "contempt for the body" apply only to people not actually in the room, and in which monologues are perfectly acceptable, because everyone's already thinking the same thing.

Which, to be fair, they are. Most contemporary American political poems are written for contemporary American poets, which means that political poems generally have more relevance to the politics of the poetry world than to the politics of America. Our avant-gardists have yet to topple capitalism by undermining narrative, but they've gotten some coveted jobs and made their way onto syllabi. Pseudo-political poems—and there are legions of them—won't unsettle anyone's assumptions about the debacle in Iraq, but they stand a good chance of being praised within the poetry community for their good intentions (much as "Bush's War" was congratulated in *The Washington Post* by Robert Pinsky for "meditat[ing] on the persistent mass violence and self-righteousness of a century"). Of course, the politics of the poetry world have their own value, and there's nothing wrong with poets behaving accordingly. But it's worth wondering whether it's always a good idea to separate political poetry from the demands of rhetoric, or declare that "all poetry is political," or equate observations about emotional states with political speech. It's worth wondering because politics is its own world, whose actors often have never heard of Wallace Stevens, much less "The Idea of Order at Key West," and whose customs must be acknowledged before they can be effectively challenged.

———

How, then, do you acknowledge those customs and that reality? This is a hard question, and one that contemporary

American poetry on the whole hasn't answered effectively. The typical response is to position oneself well outside any kind of actual power or responsibility and address the political world as if one were either a wanly sorrowing space alien, like Hass, or a lightning-eyed hermit atop some gusty bluff, like Adrienne Rich. The idea of "bearing witness" gets tossed around a good bit (as of this writing, I get 237,000 Google hits for that phrase plus "poetry"), which indicates how beside the point the notions of persuasion or conversation can seem in these discussions. When you're busy witnessing, is there really any need to talk?

But if we reach back a little further—to around 1960, say—it's possible to see how a poet might speak not just about a political subject, but within it. Gwendolyn Brooks's "The *Chicago Defender* Sends a Man to Little Rock" begins by discussing the friendly normalcy of Little Rock, the way its people "sing / Sunday hymns like anything, / Through Sunday pomp and polishing. // And after testament and tunes, / Some soften Sunday afternoons / With lemon tea and Lorna Doones." Her speaker—a journalist for the nation's largest African-American newspaper—sees around her not the stereotypes she expected, but the sadder, stranger spectacle of evil among the everyday. The poem concludes:

> I scratch my head, massage the hate-I-had.
> I blink across my prim and penciled pad.
> The saga I was sent for is not down.

Because there is a puzzle in this town.
The biggest News I do not dare
Telegraph to the Editor's chair:
"They are like people everywhere."

The angry Editor would reply
In hundred harryings of Why.

And true, they are hurling spittle, rock,
Garbage and fruit in Little Rock.
And I saw coiling storm a-writhe
On bright madonnas. And a scythe
Of men harassing brownish girls.
(The bows and barrettes in the curls
And braids declined away from joy.)

I saw a bleeding brownish boy . . .

The lariat lynch-wish I deplored.

The loveliest lynchee was our Lord.

What Brooks is doing here is very different from what
Hass is doing in "Bush's War." Brooks positions her poem
directly among the people—some black, but mostly white,
I'd guess—whom she hopes to address. Her rhymes are
brisk. Her diction is simple and approachable ("Lorna
Doones"). She anchors the poem in tetrameter couplets, one

of the oldest and most familiar verse forms (Marvell: "Had we but world enough, and time, / This coyness, lady, were no crime"). She stays within her audience's range of reference. ("Bush's War," on the other hand, includes remarks like *"Bald nur*—Goethe—no, / *Warte nur, bald ruhest du auch"*—which is the conclusion of Goethe's "Wayfarer's Night Song II" and has the practical effect of limiting the poem's audience to comp. lit. students, poetry critics, and people who get a kick out of italics.)

None of this makes Brooks's poem better than Hass's, or makes her political message more convincing (indeed, Brooks herself would later become more skeptical of the conciliatory stance adopted here). And of course, one could criticize Brooks's poem for the many things it doesn't do, such as engaging in ingenious formal maneuvers or tackling the political philosophy that undergirds the day-to-day reality being addressed. That criticism would be fair and true, and there is a place for it. But what seems plain is that "The Chicago Defender Sends a Man to Little Rock," like Nader's poem and unlike "Bush's War," has the potential to function as local, specific political speech. It doesn't assume its own powerlessness; it approaches the reader as one citizen addressing another. It aims to persuade.

———

Sometimes, however, persuasion is a matter of timing. That is, aside from the question of whether a poem is political, there is also the question of *when* a poem is political. W. H.

Auden wrote "September 1, 1939" as a rhetorical (and anti-rhetorical) response to Germany's invasion of Poland:

> I sit in one of the dives
> On Fifty-Second Street
> Uncertain and afraid
> As the clever hopes expire
> Of a low dishonest decade:
> Waves of anger and fear
> Circulate over the bright
> And darkened lands of the earth,
> Obsessing our private lives;
> The unmentionable odour of death
> Offends the September night . . .

After its political moment passed, the poem spent decades as a vague statement about being one of "the Just" who are, alas, so widely misunderstood—and Auden became annoyed enough with its self-congratulatory tone that he left it out of collections. But then, of course, came September 11, 2001, and the poem emerged again as fully political, fully connected to the spirit of a time and place (as Peter Steinfels observed in *The New York Times*, it was "endlessly quoted and reprinted to express grief over what had happened and foreboding about what was to come"). Indeed, Auden's poem has few rivals among the poetry associated with September 11. One of them, though, might be "Home to Roost" by Kay Ryan:

The chickens
are circling and
blotting out the
day. The sun is
bright, but the
chickens are in
the way. Yes,
the sky is dark
with chickens,
dense with them.
They turn and
then they turn
again. These
are the chickens
you let loose
one at a time
and small—
various breeds.
Now they have
come home
to roost—all
the same kind
at the same speed.

The only problem, of course, is that like Auden's poem, "Home to Roost" was written prior to September 11 and has nothing whatsoever to do with the attack, its aftermath, or the notorious invocation of the specific phrase "home to roost" by Jeremiah Wright, President Obama's former pastor. Ryan enjoys tweaking clichés, but when a particular cliché is thrown into political relief—as often happens—then her poem tends to follow. It'll be another five years before she can call this one her own again, which probably annoys her endlessly.

One of the problems with political poetry, then, is that like all speech, it exists at the mercy of time, history, and other people. But that doesn't mean poetry itself is passive. While it's probably true that most poets are not, as Tom Buffenbarger said, "fighters"—by which he meant "political actors"—it's also true that poems like "Home to Roost" can be less predictable. They have their own realities, and the worlds they contain cannot be lightly dismissed. And as a maker of poems, a poet is always engaged in battle, though the opponents may be unclear, the stakes unknowable, and the victories and defeats felt far away, in different domains, by people other than himself.

form

A T THE END OF the first chapter of Jonathan Kellerman's 1994 thriller, *Bad Love*, the protagonist receives a mysterious recording in the mail. He plays it and hears—brace yourself!—"throat-ripping howling interspersed with trapped-animal panting . . . I pictured a torture chamber, shrieking black mouths, convulsing bodies." What *we* hear, of course, is the familiar clockwork of the contemporary suspense novel. But watch what happens as Kellerman brings his setup to its emotional peak:

I leapt up to turn down the volume on the machine. Found it already set low.

I started to turn it off, but before I could, the screaming died.

More static-quiet.
Then a new voice.
Soft. High-pitched. Nasal.
A child's voice:

> Bad love. Bad love.
> Don't give me the bad love.

Child's timbre—but with no childish lilt.
Unnaturally flat—*robot*like.

> Bad love. Bad love.
> Don't give me the bad love . . .

Repeating it. Three times. Four.
A chant, Druidish and mournful—so oddly metallic.
Almost like a prayer.

> Bad love. Bad love . . .

No. Too hollow for prayer—too faithless.
Idolatrous.
A prayer for the dead.
By the dead.

The syntax begins breaking, the pauses between phrases
become amplified, the regular unit through which the story

had been proceeding—the three- or four-sentence paragraph—is discarded in favor of isolated lines. It's almost, one might say, like modern poetry. In fact, imagine how you might read the conclusion of the same passage if it appeared surrounded by white space in *The Atlantic Monthly* like so:

The Bad Love

More static-quiet.
Then a new voice.
Soft. High-pitched. Nasal.
A child's voice:

> *Bad love. Bad love.*
> *Don't give me the bad love.*

Child's timbre—but with no childish lilt.
Unnaturally flat—*robot*like.

> *Bad love. Bad love.*
> *Don't give me the bad love . . .*

And so on. You'd probably start reading the passage as poetry because, well, it looks like poetry. It sounds like poetry too—just compare Kellerman's lines with the following actual poem by Pulitzer Prize winner Franz Wright:

Slip

The black balloon
tied to her wrist again, thin hand
floating
an inch above the white
white sheet

The body
a word to be said
into death, one
word
which no one else knows
completely her own—

Night just the shadow of her hell

Are you sure you could tell the poem from the "poem"? This isn't to suggest that we're really reading contemporary poetry whenever we pick up an old copy of *Red Dragon*. The point is rather that many of the technical maneuvers we associate with poetry aren't unique to poetry and are more pervasive than we realize. It's important to keep this in mind, because nothing—not politics, not gossip, not the inequities of the grant application process—gets poets quite as riled up as the concept of form. Why is that?

In order to answer that question, and a few others that are

equally interesting, we first need to take a quick tour of the twentieth-century arguments about poetic form. A cartoon-ish version of that history goes something like this:

1. Prior to 1910 or so, poets generally wrote in standard meters and used traditional English forms, along with a few acceptable French and Italian cousins. If a poet wrote a sonnet, then he used pentameter just like Wordsworth did.

2. Then came modernism, and in the twinkling of an eye (or at any rate, a couple of decades), poets were sticking random bits of personal letters into their poems (as William Carlos Williams does in *Paterson*), treating random phrases as if they were complete poetic lines (as H. D. does pretty much everywhere), mucking around with Chinese translations (as Ezra Pound does, or at least thinks he does), and generally failing to adhere to traditional form.

3. After that, what happened was . . . actually, it isn't clear what happened, but W. H. Auden became the most famous poet in the English-speaking world, and he generally wrote in traditional forms. So traditional form had a comeback, maybe. In any case, the poets of the 1950s are usually talked about as if all of them wrote slightly stiff, ironic poems with regular if com-plicated stanza structures. Sometimes this gets blamed on T. S. Eliot for reasons that are confusing.

4. But *then*, fortunately, everyone realized they'd been caging their Inner Selves, and through the 1960s and 1970s, the Beats, the Black Mountain gang, the New York School, and slightly later, the Deep Image poets jettisoned regular forms in favor of long, loopy Whitmanian lines; chatty, surrealistic lines of varying length; and short, gnomic lines about snow, bones, and mystical whatnots. It was the Age of Aquarius!

5. This craziness tired everyone out, though, so by the 1980s, many poets had settled into a kind of not really metrical but also not exactly irregular poem that was smartly put together and mildly interesting— the poetic equivalent of a song by the Eagles. This framework, a standby in creative writing classes, was famously derided by the poet and critic Donald Hall as the "McPoem," which was a terrible insult because, as everyone knows, all the best poets eat at Taco Bell.

6. Still, though, we weren't quite tired of fighting about traditional forms. So a group of writers calling themselves the "New Formalists" began insisting that poets should really start writing sonnets again, neatly stepping around the fact that many poets had, in fact, been writing sonnets for decades. At more or less the same time, a bunch of writers called the Language Poets were insisting that sonnets were passé, neatly stepping around the fact that many poets had, in fact, been avoiding writing sonnets for decades. Naturally,

these two groups were much discussed, even though, as the scholar David Bromwich diplomatically put it with reference to the Language Poets, "they do not, as yet, appear to write good poems."

7. Which brings us to today. We have poets who write in traditional form (Marilyn Hacker). We have poets who don't write in traditional form (C. D. Wright). We have poets who write in forms that aren't really traditional but seem like they should be (Kay Ryan). We have poets who write in traditional form in jokey and/or disturbing ways (John Ashbery, Frederick Seidel). We have poets who write in traditional form sometimes and in various versions of free verse other times (too many poets to count). We have either a gorgeous mosaic or a big mess, depending upon whom you ask.

So there you have it. Again, this version of events is in many ways ridiculous—a competent critic could poke ninety-five holes in it in under two minutes. But this history isn't significant because it's right, it's significant because it reflects what many poetry readers say or imply when they're talking off the cuff. And our most casual and lightly held beliefs are often exactly the ones that lead us into the most intense disagreements.

In this case, those disagreements generally revolve around two opposing narratives. First, as you may have noticed from the above history, poets and poetry readers have been attracted to stories in which the art breaks through into a new style by abandoning traditional form, which is often held to represent The Past in general, and especially such pernicious aspects of the past as colonialism, empire-building, and that blue-blazered figure, The Man. It doesn't seem to faze some people that this particular story has been told several times—a fact that would seem to undercut it (the same breakthrough ought not have to be repeated every thirty years). Second, we have the counter-assertion that more recent formal approaches (like free verse) are "chaotic" or "just line-broken prose" and that traditional form represents a return to "real" poetry. Variations on these two narratives have been duking it out for ages. Consider these examples, some of which I've cribbed from David Caplan's very good introduction to his book *Questions of Possibility: Contemporary Poetry and Poetic Form*:

> [L]ike the clothing or furniture of earlier centuries, the
> verse forms of, say, the Romantic period cannot, in fact,
> be replicated except as museum curiosities . . .
>
> —MARJORIE PERLOFF, "THE OULIPO FACTOR:
> THE PROCEDURAL POETICS OF CHRISTIAN BÖK
> AND CAROLINE BERGVALL," 2003

> Free verse . . . is, I believe, happily on the decline, and
> few serious poets now bother with it. But it is still a
> very common cheap and popular substitute for poetry,

and critics of literature continue to treat it with a
consideration it does not deserve . . .

—A. D. HOPE, "FREE VERSE: A POST-MORTEM," 1965

[T]he pentameter is a dead form, and its continued use
. . . is in the strict sense reactionary.

—ANTHONY EASTHOPE, *Poetry as Discourse*, 1983

To me all sonnets say the same thing of no importance.

—WILLIAM CARLOS WILLIAMS,

INTRODUCTION TO *Collected Poems*, 1944

And just for fun, and to give you a sense of how long this
sort of thing has been going on:

[The sonnet] is not very suitable to the English
language, and has not been used by any man of
eminence since Milton.

—SAMUEL JOHNSON,

A Dictionary of the English Language, 1755

As you can see, the same problems have been abounding
for quite a while now. If pentameter is indeed a dead form,
then what do we do about the fact that poets are writing in it,
have been writing in it, and probably will be writing in it for
the foreseeable future? By the same token, though, if there
is a proper way to write in form that we've deserted, how do

we explain the fact that readers have been happily reading these improper forms as forms for decades? Has everyone just been wrong all along?

Perhaps. Or maybe the difficulty lies not with all the wrongheaded people who refuse to cooperate with our theories, and rather with the assumptions about the nature of form that support those theories. What, after all, is a poetic form? To judge from the quotations above, it seems that while a piece of writing might itself be complicated, the form of that writing is relatively straightforward stuff. Sure, one might struggle to write a sonnet, or one might have a hard time interpreting someone else's sonnet, but the concept "writing a sonnet" isn't hard to understand at all. After all, we have fixed rules that tell us how to go about it. And it follows that producing a new form is simply a matter of tinkering around with those rules—as a young computer programmer might have tinkered around in a Silicon Valley garage circa 1980—until *voila*, one has discovered the poetic equivalent of Linux.

The problem, however, is that our rules turn out to be not quite as clear as we think. Here it's helpful to return briefly to Jonathan Kellerman. Why do Kellerman's lines seem poetic when we set them off from the rest of his text? Well, they look like poetry, one might say—we recognize that's how we should read them. But it's not quite enough simply to take note of what we're seeing, as we might take note of a car approaching as we're about to cross the street. As the philosopher Kendall Walton points out in making a related argument about artistic genres and styles, "Recognition is a momentary occurrence, whereas perceiving a quality is a continuous state which may last for a short or long time." When we read a poem as a sonnet, we aren't just thinking, "Bingo, a sonnet!"; we're thinking back to past sonnets we've read, to information we know about sonnets broadly speaking, to dozens of features of the poem in front of us, and to associations we have with sonnets, poems, and poetry generally. We might think, "Bingo, a sonnet!"; and then, five seconds later, "Actually, no bingo, it's not looking much like a sonnet anymore"; and then, five seconds after that, "Okay, it's sort of sonnet-ish in the middle bits." We're in a state of perceiving, and blurry perceiving at that.

Words like "blurry" are, of course, unsatisfying. We like the clean edges of clear concepts, whether we're playing baseball or doing our taxes or reading poems. But it's a mistake to let that desire lead us into frames of mind that make poems less interesting than they can be. And here it's worth repeating a point I touched on earlier: There's no aspect of poetry more significant than form (according to some critics, poetry is nothing *but* form), and consequently no aspect of poetry more likely to lead to confusion and unhappiness among poets and poetry readers. This means that while it may seem needlessly abstract to be talking about "recognition" and "perception" and so forth—when of course what we really want to know are things like "Is it still okay to like sonnets, or what?"—it's essential to look at the basic questions first, because they're exactly the ones that can trip us up later.

So what are we really talking about when we're talking about poetic form? Before we look at that question more specifically, let me clarify a general matter: The idea of form I'm discussing here is slightly different from related notions like "style" and "shape." When I say, "This poem has form X," I don't just mean that the poem looks or sounds a certain way; rather, I mean that there's some distinct, often nameable category called "X" that we think (and we think the poet thinks) we're supposed to recognize as being associated with the poem, and that we could imagine being associated with other poems as well. That sounds complicated, but in practice the difference between form and ideas like "shape" is relatively straightforward. Consider, for instance, the beginning of Louise Glück's "The Drowned Children":

> You see, they have no judgment.
> So it is natural that they should drown,
> first the ice taking them in
> and then, all winter, their wool scarves
> floating behind them as they sink
> until at last they are quiet.
> And the pond lifts them in its manifold dark arms.
>
> But death must come to them differently,
> so close to the beginning.
> As though they had always been

blind and weightless. Therefore
the rest is dreamed, the lamp,
the good white cloth that covered the table,
their bodies.

This is fine writing, but it isn't *formal* writing as we usu-
ally mean it. That's not to say Glück's poem doesn't have
something we might call a structure, or that it doesn't have
other distinguishing linguistic properties. Yet if you were to
say to a group of poets, "Please write a poem in the form of
'Drowned Children,'" there wouldn't be general agreement
about what you were asking for. A poet could imitate Glück's
style—the austere diction ("good white cloth"), the com-
posed, chilly tone—but the actual form of the poem seems
curiously absent, or at least hard to name. This is because
we've come to think of pieces of writing like "Drowned Chil-
dren" not as "poems with form X," but simply as "poems."

The easiest way to appreciate this odd but significant
distinction is to consider the concept of parody. In order to
be effective, a parody has to involve categories we actually
understand and acknowledge—no one, for example, is go-
ing to get a joke based on the structure of early Etruscan
comedy—which means that a parody that involves contem-
porary poetic form must include a form that we recognize
as such. To understand the consequences this point has for
the present discussion, let's look quickly at two different pa-
rodic poems. The first, by the journalist Hart Seely, is called

"Happenings" and consists entirely of remarks delivered by
Donald Rumsfeld in a 2003 press briefing:

> You're going to be told lots of things.
> You get told things every day that don't happen.
>
> It doesn't seem to bother people, they don't—
> It's printed in the press.
> The world thinks all these things happen.
> They never happened.
>
> Everyone's so eager to get the story
> Before in fact the story's there
> That the world is constantly being fed
> Things that haven't happened.
>
> All I can tell you is,
> It hasn't happened.
> It's going to happen.

There are two things to notice in particular about this
poem. First, as I hope you can see, it sounds a bit like
"Drowned Children." Second, if you were to ask people
why this piece of writing is funny, they'd likely say some-
thing about it being "a poem." It's unlikely, however, that
they would say they found it funny because it's a special
form of poem; they wouldn't, for instance, say it's funny

"because it's free verse." Contrast that with how most readers responded to the resignation of Sun Microsystems CEO Jonathan Schwartz in early 2010, which was submitted via Twitter like so:

Financial crisis
Stalled too many customers
CEO no more

Is this funny because it's a poem? No, it's funny because it's a haiku—its humor depends specifically on the recognition of that form. We view haiku as a distinctive category of poetry in a way that we do not, for various reasons, recognize the structure or shape of "Drowned Children."

———

So when we're talking about form, we're often talking about categories of categories. This can make for a confusing conversation, obviously. But we can simplify things somewhat by sorting our contemporary ideas about form into three loose groupings, each of which can (and often does) overlap with one or both of the others. Those categories are:

1. Metrical Form
2. Resemblance Form
3. Mechanical Form

With the exception of meter, these are descriptions of my own invention, so if you're seated beside a poet on a plane and ask if he writes a lot of "resemblance forms," he's not going to know what you're talking about. But these general categories do, I think, manage to summarize the manner in which most poets actually conceive of form today, even if they sometimes disagree with conventional critical wisdom. So let's look at each in slightly more detail.

Metrical Form

In English, meter is the structuring of poetry around stress difference; or to put it another way:

> In **Eng**lish, **me**ter **is** the **struc**tur**ing**
> of **po**etry a**round stress dif**fer**ence**.

In other languages, meter can be a little different, as *The New Princeton Encyclopedia of Poetry and Poetics* makes explicit, if not necessarily plain:

> [M]eter selects one phonological feature of language
> (stress, pitch, length) and reduces it several levels
> or degrees in ordinary speech . . . to a simple binary
> opposition . . . which may be generalized as "marked"
> versus "unmarked." Regular patterns of these
> contrastive features create units of structure . . . which
> in turn comprise the line of verse.

So meter involves creating a two-part division in something like stress (English), tone (Chinese), or syllable length (ancient Greek), and then using that contrast to create various effects. The easiest way to understand meter, though, is simply to hear it in action, as in the conclusion to Tennyson's "Ulysses":

To strive, to seek, to find, and not to yield.
da DUM da DUM da DUM da DUM da DUM

Meters vary, of course, so we find a very different arrangement in *Macbeth*:

Double, double, toil and trouble
DUM da DUM da DUM da DUM da

And yet another sort in Dr. Seuss's *The Lorax*:

He was   very   upset as   he shouted and puffed
da da   DUM da   da DUM da   da DUM da   da DUM

There are already many good books on meter available, so I won't spend time here going over the intricacies of anapestic tetrameter or trochaic dimeter (suffice it to say they're complicated and worth learning about). For the present discussion, only a few things are worth noting. The first is simply that American poets have worked in meter since the country's creation, and they continue to do so today, despite the wishes of some of our more proscriptive critics. Here, for instance, is the beginning of A. E. Stallings's sonnet "Sine Qua Non" from 2006, which is written in richly varied iambic pentameter:

> Your absence, father, is nothing. It is naught—
> The factor by which nothing will multiply,
> The gap of a dropped stitch, the needle's eye
> Weeping its black thread. It is the spot
> Blindly spreading through the looking glass.
> It is the startled silences that come
> When the refrigerator stops its hum,
> And crickets pause to let the winter pass.

Stallings's poem helps make another point worth bearing in mind about meter, which is that it's more complicated and less predictable than you might expect (only the last line above is "strictly" iambic: "And **crick**ets **pause** to **let** the **win**ter **pass**"). The underlying pattern of a given meter is fixed, but the maneuvers that can be made within and against that set pattern are, if not infinite, certainly abundant.

The last thing to be said about metrical writing is that it necessarily occupies an unusual position in any discussion of form in general. This is the case for several reasons. Meter is an aural phenomenon (we "hear" it as we read), whereas many other formal structures—sonnets, for instance—are perceived visually. Meter is also vastly older and larger than other aspects of form; as the *Princeton Encyclopedia* notes, "the preponderance of all poetry written in the history of the world has been metrical." But perhaps the most peculiar and interesting thing about meter may be the extent to which it lends itself to linguistic analysis. Although linguists are still arguing about what meter is and how it works, many agree that, as the scholar Kristin Hanson puts it,

> . . . a poet composing in a given meter has intuitions as to what is possible within the form, in the same way that a speaker has intuitions about what is grammatical in his or her language. Hence, a meter is similarly the knowledge of the rules, articulated or not, that govern those intuitions and generate the variety of surface rhythms manifest in the lines of individual poems in the meter . . . [T]he question arises as to whether there can be a general theory of meter, constraining the form of such rules and accounting for the variety of them found across languages.

So there's at least the possibility of a broad theory of meter that would encompass metrical variations in English, Finnish, and Japanese. Whether or not such a theory is ever perfected, the fact that it's even discussed indicates the extent to which meter differs from other formal categories (no one, for instance, has yet suggested that we might one day have a cross-cultural theory of limericks). Moreover, as Hanson notes, many linguists believe that meter is rule-governed within a given poet's body of work, allowing us to make relatively clear statements about what is or isn't metrical in a particular passage. It's important to note, however, that our ability to define a set of rules for meter has little effect on the way we actually go about perceiving metrical effects in a given piece of writing. Our interpretation of literary form is, as I've said, a blurry business. No matter how exact we can be about the formal model under discussion, the perception of that model is inevitably a matter of weighing various pieces of evidence, and then reaching conclusions that can vary in strength about how the writing looks or sounds.

Resemblance Form

Which brings us, appropriately enough, to the idea of resemblance. A resemblance form is one that we associate with a poem not because the poem follows a certain set of rules, but because the poem resembles other poems we've previously identified with the form in question. Resemblance forms are things like sonnets, villanelles, sestinas, rondeaux, and so forth—basically, the arsenal of the creative writing exercise book. In characterizing these forms in this manner, I'm borrowing from the linguist Nigel Fabb, whose *Language and Literary Structure* is among the best books I've read on poetic form, including (sadly) almost all books written by actual poets. Fabb puts forms like the sonnet into a category he calls "variable form" (for various reasons, I prefer "resemblance form"), which he describes in this way:

> Because these kinds of form hold to a certain degree
> rather than holding invariably, they cannot be
> generated by rule . . . These variable kinds of form
> hold of a text only by virtue of being the content of
> weaker or stronger thoughts about the text.

That may sound complicated, but in practice what Fabb is suggesting is reasonably straightforward. Unlike meter, the sonnet can't be described in terms of linguistic rules; instead, it exists only as the result of a series of inferences we make about a given piece of writing. We think, "This poem has fourteen lines, so it might be a sonnet," or, "This poem is titled 'Sonnet,' so it might be a sonnet," and so forth. Ultimately we arrive at a conclusion about the "sonnetness" of what we're looking at, and that conclusion can be of greater or lesser strength. So it makes perfect sense, for instance, to say that a particular poem is "loosely" a sonnet.

There are several interesting consequences that come from looking at forms like the sonnet in this way. The first, of course, is that the idea of resemblance allows us to get around the always problematic question of rules for such poems. Simply put, there are no rules for resemblance-based poetic forms. Or rather, there are no rules according to the usual way in which we think about rules, which is to say as almost physical steps that may be taken rightly or wrongly, but not wrongly rightly or rightly wrongly. A resemblance form isn't something one gets from following a formula; rather, it's a quality we can attribute to a piece of writing.

This may surprise you. Possibly you remember getting a B- in third grade because your haiku had a 5-7-4 syllable pattern, instead of ending on the Absolutely Required Five Syllables. And yet here is former poet laureate Robert Hass translating one of Kobayashi Issa's haiku:

> Don't worry, spiders,
> I keep house
>   casually

It's not even close to 5-7-5! But it's lovely, and it sure seems like a haiku, doesn't it? The question, then, is if we should reject what is probably our initial notion—*This is a haiku*—because of the failure of the poem to adhere to the syllable count we've been told is necessary. On one hand, 5-7-5 seems like a clear standard that plainly hasn't been met. On the other hand, again, Hass's poem certainly looks like a haiku—and since an English syllable isn't actually the equivalent of the sound unit used to compose Japanese haiku, the 5-7-5 count can be no better than an approximation of the original version (on top of that, the haiku is one vertical line in Japanese, not three horizontal lines). So because the haiku is a relatively young form taken from another culture, it seems reasonable to assume its "rules," if that's what they are, can still be contested.

But there are better and more subtle reasons for thinking that rule-governance isn't a good model for forms like haikus and sonnets. The first, as Fabb points out, is the idea of degree or intensity. Resemblance has no trouble allowing for degree—just think of how one sibling may strongly have the family "look," while another sibling may show it only weakly. But rule-based systems aren't very good with degrees; usually you've either obeyed the rule, or you haven't. That inflexibility can be a problem when we're talking about forms like sonnets, because it turns out that almost every rule has an exception. If, for example, we say that sonnets must have fourteen lines, then we need to account for Shakespeare's Sonnet 99 (fifteen lines), Shakespeare's Sonnet 126 (twelve lines), all fifty of George Meredith's sonnets in *Modern Love* (sixteen lines), Gerard Manley Hopkins's "Pied Beauty" (either eleven lines or ten and a half, depending on how you look at it), Yeats's "He Wishes His Beloved Were Dead" (thirteen lines), and on and on.

Moreover, poems are always read in the context of other poems. When we say, for instance, "William Meredith's poem 'The Illiterate' is a sonnet," we mean that "The Illiterate" belongs to the very large array of English-language sonnets that extends from the sonnet's emergence in the early sixteenth century to, well, right this minute. But poems are also often part of specific local contexts, and if we cling to the notion that forms like the sonnet are determined by rules, then we have trouble explaining a peculiar phenomenon that can occur in such arrangements. By this, I mean that particular groupings of poems can make us more inclined to attach a form to an individual poem than we would be if the poem were presented in isolation. Again, this is a concept best demonstrated by example. The conclusion of Paul Muldoon's ingenious and disturbing book *Quoof* is a sequence of fifty poems called "The More a Man Has the More a Man Wants" that reinterprets the Native American trickster cycle as a series of bizarre incidents involving a dodgy character named Gallogly. The poems are uniformly fourteen lines, and it's pretty plain they should be read as sonnets—which isn't a problem, since most of them satisfy contemporary interpretations of the form reasonably well. But after forty-seven such poems, Muldoon delivers this:

Just
throw
him
a
cake
of
Sunlight
soap,
let
him
wash
him-
self
ashore.

Taken on its own, this slender poem probably wouldn't be seen by many readers as a sonnet. But surrounded by forty-nine poems that we *would* read independently as sonnets, it's hard not to feel that something sonnetish is going on. This isn't a response that can be easily accommodated by rules, but the theory of resemblance has no trouble accounting for it. Sometimes, you don't know how much a person takes after his family until you see him with the right configuration of aunts and uncles.

That said, it seems reasonable to suppose that some resemblance-based effects can be trickier to manage than others. The sestina, for instance, usually involves six six-line stanzas followed by a tercet, with the same six end words being used in each stanza. Surely, one might think, there are only a few ways a poem can "look" while still encouraging us to have the thought "This is a sestina." Likewise, the villanelle is typically characterized by heavy rhyming and two alternating refrains, as the opening of Dylan Thomas's famous "Do Not Go Gentle Into That Good Night" demonstrates:

> Do not go gentle into that good night,
> Old age should burn and rave at close of day;
> Rage, rage against the dying of the light.
>
> Though wise men at their end know dark is right,
> Because their words had forked no lightning they
> Do not go gentle into that good night.

Good men, the last wave by, crying how bright
Their frail deeds might have danced in a green bay,
Rage, rage against the dying of the light . . .

Is there any way to write refrains without writing re-
frains? Or to put things a little more abstractly, when a form
is this distinctly regimented—with strict repetitions, and so
forth—does it really make sense to insist that it's based on
resemblance, rather than on a set of rules? The short answer
is: Yes, actually. The longer answer is that while a poet may
have to work a bit harder to create an effective "loose" resem-
blance in some situations, even the strictest-seeming forms of
this sort are matters of evocation and interpretation. Con-
sider Thomas Sayers Ellis's "Atomic Bride," which begins:

A good show
Starts in the
Dressing room

And works its way
To the stage.
Close the door,

Andre's cross-
dressing, what
A drag. All

The world loves
A bride, something
About those gowns.

A good wedding
Starts in the
Department store

And works its way
Into the photo album.
Close the door,

Andre's tying
The knot, what
A drag. Isn't he

Lovely? All
The world loves
A bachelor, some-

thing about glamour
& glitz, white
Shirts, lawsuits.

A good dog
Starts in the yard

And works its way
Into da house . . .

Can you see the resemblance yet? If not, how about if we
rearrange the poem like so:

A good show starts in the dressing room and works its
    way
To the stage. Close the door, Andre's cross-dressing,
What a drag. All the world loves

A bride, something about those gowns.
A good wedding
Starts in the department store and works its way

Into the photo album.
Close the door, Andre's tying the knot, what
A drag. Isn't he lovely? All the world loves

A bachelor, something about glamour
& glitz, white shirts, lawsuits. A good dog
Starts in the yard and works its way

Into da house . . .

Once you see that the repetitive elements in Ellis's poem
are working together as alternating refrains, it's hard to
avoid thinking "villanelle," even if "Atomic Bride" doesn't

register the form as strongly as "Do Not Go Gentle Into That Good Night." Like reading a sonnet, reading a villanelle is a matter of appreciating an affinity, not making a determination according to a checklist.

Mechanical Form

There is, however, another general category of form that's much less averse to things like checklists. This is the very loose grouping that I've chosen to call "mechanical form," which is similar in some ways to what is occasionally referred to as "constrained writing." If resemblance forms are united by the idea that the writer will create a likeness that the reader can recognize, mechanical forms are connected to each other by a shared emphasis on the writing process itself. Again, this is a definition perhaps best demonstrated by example. Here is the opening of Gilbert Adair's translation of Georges Perec's *A Void*:

> Today, by radio, and also on giant hoardings, a rabbi, an admiral notorious for his links to Masonry, a trio of cardinals, a trio, too, of insignificant politicians (bought and paid for by a rich and corrupt Anglo-Saxon banking corporation), inform us all of how our country now risks dying of starvation.

Notice anything? Possibly not, which is a tribute to Perec's and Adair's ingenuity. Because the entire passage,

and indeed the entire 280-page novel, is missing the letter
"e." *A Void* is therefore what's known as a lipogram: a liter-
ary work in which one or more letters is deliberately omitted
in composition.

This is the essence of mechanical writing. A mechanical
form involves a simple rule based on inclusion, exclusion,
counting, or some similar procedure, and the poems gener-
ated according to the rule in question can vary widely—one
lipogram doesn't necessarily look like any other lipogram.
In addition, mechanical forms typically don't allow for the
idea of degree: A lipogram that fails to obey its governing
rule doesn't register as a "loose" lipogram; it just seems like
a mistake. Because our awareness of the rule governing the
text's creation is so important to our appreciation of a me-
chanical form, a large part of the pleasure of such poetry de-
pends not on the text itself, but on the reader's awareness of
the difficulty, awkwardness, and occasional hilarity of the
writing process. This is perhaps why, in its most severe in-
carnations, mechanical form can be simultaneously dazzling
and painful to read. For instance, here's a two-part poem by
Bonita C. Miller from 1974 that I ran across in a review of
Ross Eckler's *Making the Alphabet Dance*:

The Cynic's Soliloquy; Her Reply

Wit: howl on, gibe: rate the semen
Of thy men "waste." Stedfast—be low!

Be foul, men, ever. No moralist and
Ho! nor able to go do good.

With Ow! long I berate these men.
Oft hymen was tested fast below.
Befoul me never. No; moral I stand,
Honorable to God. O, good.

The rule governing this poem is, as you may have noticed, that each line contains exactly the same letters in exactly the same order as its corresponding line in the other section. The only thing that varies is punctuation. My own response to this poem hovers somewhere between impressed at the time this must have taken to write, and being depressed by the time this must have taken to write.

Yet if mechanical forms can sometimes seem overdetermined, they can also have a peculiar appeal, especially when the governing rule is more open-ended. The cento, for example, is a form originating in ancient Greece that is constructed entirely from lines or pieces of lines from other poems. David Lehman's "Oxford Cento," which he composed after editing the *Oxford Book of American Poetry*, begins:

If the sun shines but approximately
Only where love and need are one,
Who in this Bowling Alley bowld the Sun?
Of whom shall we speak? For every day they die

Younger than their kids—jeans, ski-pants, sneakers.
And the stars never rise but I see the bright eyes
Waking far apart on the bed, the two of them.
And so it was I entered the broken world.

The quotations are from, in order, Laura Riding, Robert Frost, Edward Taylor, W. H. Auden, James Merrill, Edgar Allan Poe, John Ashbery, and Hart Crane—but like most good centos, the poem feels very much its own creation. Similarly, syllabic verse, which is simply poetry written according to a strict syllable count, can be every bit as supple as the freest free verse. Here's Thom Gunn's "My Sad Captains," which is limited to seven syllables per line:

One by one they appear in
the darkness: a few friends, and
a few with historical
names. How late they start to shine!
but before they fade they stand
perfectly embodied, all

the past lapping them like a
cloak of chaos. They were men
who, I thought, lived only to
renew the wasteful force they
spent with each hot convulsion.
They remind me, distant now.

True, they are not at rest yet,
but now that they are indeed
apart, winnowed from failures,
they withdraw to an orbit
and turn with disinterested
hard energy, like the stars.

Like all forms, mechanical forms give the poet an extra
tool for communicating meaning, and that meaning is no less
effective for being explicitly rule bound.

———————

Now, of course, having spent eighteen pages carefully outlin-
ing three approaches to formalism, I have to confess: These
categories are barely categories. Indeed, to call them perme-
able would be putting it mildly—meter, resemblance form,
and mechanical form aren't distinct groupings so much as ar-
eas of occasional concentration, with many poems combining
elements from two or even all three of these concepts. Con-
sider the following sonnet, which, like the poem by Bonita
Miller on page 88, appears in *Making the Alphabet Dance*:

Washington Crossing the Delaware

A hard, howling, tossing, water scene:
Strong tide was washing hero clean.
"How cold!" Weather stings as in anger.
O silent night shows war ace danger!

The cold waters swashing on in rage.
Redcoats warn slow his hint engage.
When general's star action wish'd "Go!"
He saw his ragged continentals row.

Ah, he stands—sailor crew went going,
And so this general watches rowing.
He hastens—Winter again grows cold;
A wet crew gain Hessian stronghold.

George can't lose war with 's hands in;
He's astern—so, go alight, crew, and win!

Each line is, of course, an anagram of the poem's title, putting "Washington Crossing the Delaware" firmly in the camp of mechanical form. But it's also indisputably, if awkwardly, a sonnet. Nor is this poem's hybrid formal identity all that unusual—a similar, if less rigid mixture can be found in the work of poets like Paul Muldoon and Ted Berrigan (whose book *The Sonnets* uses a kind of self-cannibalizing collage to create a memorably odd sonnet sequence). And even Marianne Moore, America's most famous practitioner of syllabic verse, occasionally violated her own patterns. "What Are Years," for instance, is often held up as a classic syllabic poem, yet its twenty-fourth line is missing a syllable. Does that make it a resemblance form?

So the taxonomy I've offered here is by no means hard edged. You may also have noticed that I passed over the various forms of visual poetry (for example, poems such as George Herbert's "Easter Wings," in which the words are arranged on the page to form a pair of wings). My goal hasn't been to cover all aspects of form exhaustively, but simply to give you a sense of how complicated our idea of form is, and consequently how mistaken we would be to think that form's many aspects can be precisely characterized.

As I mentioned at the beginning of this chapter, however, we aren't always fond of fluidity and complexity. In particular we have a tendency to treat all sorts of form as if they involved the systematic application of rules that I limit here to mechanical forms. In part, I think this has to do with the extent to which poetry, like several other humanistic disciplines, has fallen under the sway of metaphors relating to science. A poet is "innovative." Poems are "experimental." A new book has "the thrill of discovery." If you're used to thinking like this, then it's easy to regard form as something that can be isolated like a compound and then tested with reagents according to a formula. And of course, the idea of strictly rule-based form is appealing to two small but vocal subsets of the poetry world. The first are people who want to have rules so that they can then fault poets for disobeying them; the second are people who want to have rules so that they can define forms more clearly, and thereby more easily consign them to some past historical period.

But a form, even a mechanical form, is bigger than the sum of its rules. A form isn't a schematic, but a practice—and in this sense, form can be compared to a game (to borrow from Wittgenstein). Think, for example, about baseball. We all know, roughly, what the Official Rules of Major League Baseball are at any given moment, or at least we can look them up online at mlb.com. But those rules change. And the idea of playing baseball turns out to be much larger than whatever the official rules of MLB are at any point in time. Intramural baseball is baseball, even if its rules are different. Hitting a ball in the street with friends might be baseball. Playing baseball on the Nintendo Wii—is that baseball? It's at least debatably so, I'd say. Forms like the sonnet inhabit this same uncertain space, and that may explain their remarkable persistence.

This is not to say, of course, that forms can never vanish. They can and do. But as long as someone is playing the game of the form in question, we should be careful about assuming that game is no bigger than the rules we happen to know or like best. Consider, for example, the following exchange from the Poetry Foundation website in late 2007. Several poets were debating the concept of the sonnet, and the Canadian writer Christian Bök (who writes almost entirely in mechanical forms) declared the sonnet to be an "obsolete literary genre." Bök then went on, however, to praise a sonnet by Karen Volkman as "absolutely exquisite" because in Bök's view, Volkman had demonstrated "lingual novelty" and "radicalize[d] the form." The sonnet in question is metrically regular, is composed of fourteen lines, uses real words, and has a traditional rhyme scheme—but it doesn't make sense and is grammatically incoherent. It's perhaps not surprising, therefore, that the poet Annie Finch tartly responded to Bök: "It is not strictly accurate to say, Christian, that Volkman's poem 'radicalizes the form of the sonnet.' In fact, it radicalizes the style of the sonnet. Maybe one could say that in doing so, it radicalizes the form by association, but the truth is that it is utterly conservative in form." Finch meant, of course, that Bök had chosen to ignore every aspect of the form except the one that he favored, and she was, I think, largely correct in her judgment (although she was perhaps wrong to call the poem's style "radical," considering that as a friend of mine pointed out, "the diction is weirdly selected for the highly 'poetic' and ends up sounding like extreme Dante Gabriel Rossetti"). But better than trying to walk the fine line between form and style, one could simply say: The sonnet is a complex game, and the ingenuity of any given performance will always depend on your position in the field. Here is Volkman's poem:

Blank bride of the hour, occluded thought
wed to waning like a sifting scent
of future flowers, retrograde intent
backwards blooming as a nascent naught
staining minutes, rumorous, uncaught.

You callow hollow of the efferent,
the apsis-axis of my implement,
ague body, unboundaried, portionless plot
no chart remarks. My paltry pretty, go
blanch your blossoms (the radix of a rot)
in some white wind some nightness stanches, stale
negative lumen of a spectral no.
What center cinches your orbit's knot,
the far aphelion of a darkest veil?

Without bothering too much over whether this is "modern" or "experimental" or "radical" or "proper" or whatever, it's worth asking: Is this interesting? Is it a sonnet? It's both, I would say—and that is enough.

ambition

WHAT IS THE SITUATION of American poetry? It's a reasonable question to ask before getting more deeply involved in the details of poems, much as it would be reasonable to ask about the situation of Belgium before deciding to go there for your birthday. Indeed, it's tempting to try to answer such a question with one of the brisk adjectives the president typically uses to describe the state of the union in his annual address to Congress. For example: "The situation of American poetry is good!" Or: "The situation is strong!" Or even, since we're talking about poems and can therefore wax eloquent: "The situation is of an empyrean magnificence! Forsooth!"

But whatever we say probably will be of limited usefulness, because like most complex systems, poetry doesn't lend itself to these sorts of summaries. What's the situation of music, for example? Well, which music do you mean? What's the situation of the ocean? Well, it's wet, but aside from that, it's tricky to generalize. By the same token, poetry is a chaotic, fluid art form—should its "situation" be defined as the situation experienced by the most poets? Or the best poets? How many of the best poets? The closer we get to being able to make a judgment about a local, specific aspect of the art— for example, that the situation of poets under the age of forty is "promising"—the further we've traveled from poetry writ large. To add to the confusion, any observation we make about poetry's situation ends up affecting that situation, because the art form's position isn't a physical fact but a temporary agreement. If we say that poetry is in "dire shape," we've helped make the art form into something about which dire pronouncements get made.

But beyond all this, poetry's "situation" is hard to describe because there seems to be little agreement—right now, at least—about what poets ought to be doing in the first place. For instance, consider the following opening lines from recent books of contemporary poetry:

Jealousy? Homage? Longing? Superstition?

An orange radio is all I need

sus: picious

Years ago, while studying Chinese art, and granted
 access to the innards of the museum, I found myself
 holding a pot over 6,000 years old.

Don't speak!

one in ruins *[and the phrase "one in ruins" is surrounded
 by Wite-Out]*

The practice keyboard teaches only fingering.

For lack of which / we put ourselves / in a cop's place

In a gondola above the Dolomites, / I turned to you
 and said, "You are / my reason for being alive."

Finally, and perhaps my favorite:

I saved part of the infection in a small plastic bag

It's especially difficult to talk about the situation of poetry
when the people writing it appear to agree on little, except
possibly that a poem should begin with words (or in the case
of the third example, a word skewered by a colon). What
was the situation of the Tower of Babel? Confusion, sayeth
the Lord.

———

So why are we confused about what it means to write a poem? That's a hard question, the answer to which has to do with political history, educational changes, cultural shifts, and probably, like everything else in the world, Google. In any case, it's complicated stuff, and more than would be practical to take on here. So instead, it might be helpful to come at the situation of poetry sideways by talking about a related concept. It might be interesting to think not about what poetry is, but about what we want it to be—to consider, that is, what it means for a poet to be *ambitious*.

This is easier said than done, though, because ambition itself is a complicated and occasionally contradictory notion. In particular, our conception of ambition implicates two things that are seemingly incompatible—incompleteness and achievement. By "incompleteness" I mean that the word "ambition" is often used to indicate a desire for accomplishment, which necessarily means that the accomplishment in question hasn't yet been reached. The ambitious person is the one who is in the process of trying to become something bigger/better/more important. And we typically associate this kind of ambition with other concepts that involve incompleteness, like youth or low rank: Rookies are ambitious, whereas veterans tend to be "hardened," "savvy," "wily," "masterful," "cool under fire," etc. As you can see, this aspect of ambition emphasizes the position of the person relative to his or her goal, which means that the nature of the goal itself is less important—the treasurer of the local birdwatchers' club can have the "ambition" of becoming the president.

But ambition also frequently involves (or at least strongly implies) a *type* of achievement, not simply a desire. More specifically, ambition is usually associated with an ideal of "greatness"—and since you can probably hear the implied capitalization, let's go ahead and call it "Greatness." The idea here is not that the person is in a lower position and seeking to rise higher, but that the project itself seems to be of tremendous scale. The classic example of this aspect of ambition in poetry is *Paradise Lost*, in which Milton informs us on the first page that he's going to "justify the ways of God to men" and then launches into a three-hundred-page version of exactly that. Had Milton said that he was going to "provide the most detailed description of a radish ever attempted in any language," that likely wouldn't strike many people as ambitious, no matter how serious he was or how hard he worked at it. Radishes just aren't that big.

So ambition involves both a kind of striving and a conception of "Greatness," and in this vague, mixed notion there's also usually a suggestion of youth. As you might expect, these ideas about ambition rub off on each other in confusing ways. Surely, for instance, it's not "ambitious" to want to win the Trumansburg Family Center miniature golf tournament—but what if you're only five years old? Is it "ambitious" to want to become an exceptionally skillful mugger? How about a competitive eating champion? Ambition implies scale, so certainly

Mount Rushmore was an ambitious project. But what if we replaced the faces of the presidents with the faces of Carrot Top, Papa Smurf, Dolph Lundgren, and the first person listed in the Des Moines phone book? These are the kind of questions that our muddled notion of ambition struggles to encompass. And in poetry, the situation can become especially confused, because we can never be entirely sure whether we're talking about the ambition of poets or the ambition of poems, or whether these two things are actually (or only sometimes) one and the same.

———

Still, however blurry "ambition" may be, it's clear that segments of the poetry world have been fretting over its potential loss since at least 1983. That's the year in which an essay by Donald Hall, the U.S. poet laureate from 2006 to 2007, appeared in the *Kenyon Review* bearing the title "Poetry and Ambition." Hall got right to the point: "[I]t seems to me that contemporary American poetry is afflicted by modesty of ambition—a modesty, alas, genuine . . . if sometimes accompanied by vast pretense." What poets should be trying to do, according to Hall, was "to make words that live forever . . . to be as good as Dante." They probably would fail, of course, but even so, "the only way we are likely to be any good is to try to be as great as the best." Pretty strong stuff—and one wonders how many plays Shakespeare would have managed to write had he subjected every line to the merciless scrutiny Hall recommends.

And yet many of Hall's points are still being wrangled over more than twenty years later. In 2005, *Poetry* magazine published a roundtable discussion entitled (naturally) "Ambition and Greatness," in which participants were alternately put off by the entire idea of "capital-G Greatness" (as the poet Daisy Fried put it) or concerned that, as the scholar Jeredith Merrin suggested, the contemporary poetry world might be trying "to rewrite 'great' as small." In general, the panelists were understandably confused over what it means to be "ambitious," and by extension, what it might mean to be "Great." For instance, here's how the first participant, the very sharp poet and critic Adam Kirsch, opens the discussion:

> A famous anecdote has it that when W. H. Auden was a student at Oxford, his tutor asked him what career he planned to pursue. He explained that he wanted to be a poet, and was met with the kind of patronizing smile all poets know so well. "You don't understand," Auden retorted, "I mean to be a great poet." One way of approaching our discussion of greatness and ambition in poetry is to ask whether any young poet today, similarly patronized, would risk Auden's reply.

This seems like a reasonable question at first, but it becomes increasingly curious the more you look at it. Because Kirsch isn't asking, "What young poet today would be as ambitious as Auden *in the writing of his poems?*" No, he's asking, "What young poet would say, *outside of his poems,* that he wanted to be 'Great'?'" Talking about ambition is being conflated with ambition itself. Think of it this way: If Auden had never said anything about wanting to be "a great poet," but had gone on to produce exactly the same books, would we have found the accomplishment any less impressive? Presumably not, yet this is the implication of the anecdote.

So what explains this odd maneuver? The answer, I think, has to do with the fact that readers are often less interested in a poem's destination than in the clarity of its road signs. We want a signal that tells us, "Here is ambition! Here is Greatness!"—and to take this point to its logical extreme, we want a signal that tells us, "Here is poetry!" These are understandable things to want, but they aren't obtainable for the same reason that the situation of poetry is always unknowable: There is no outside position that can give us perspective on a system that not only is enormous and protean, but that we ourselves inhabit. Yet if our ideas about poetic ambition are often mistaken or confused, those ideas can nonetheless have real consequences for poets and poetry. If, as I've suggested, we have a tendency to believe that ambition will be found beneath a placard reading AMBITION, then we're necessarily going to become very interested in signs. And in the context of the poetry world, this means that we're going to become very interested in styles.

———

within the orbit of Ezra Pound and Robert Frost" and "been part of that coincidence of brilliant, troubled writers . . . Theodore Roethke, Sylvia Plath, Randall Jarrell, John Berryman." No mention of Bishop was to be found. Indeed, even Bishop's 1979 obituary in *The New York Times* acknowledged that she "was less widely known than contemporaries such as Robert Lowell," whose own obituary was nearly double the length of Bishop's and appeared on the newspaper's front page (Bishop got page 13 of the B section). Bishop was by no means scorned, of course—she received major prizes and was reviewed favorably on a regular basis—but very few contemporary critics considered her to be Lowell's equal. And almost nobody thought she might be his superior.

That's not the case anymore. Shortly after the poets' deaths in the late 1970s, the reputation of Lowell began to sink, the reputation of Bishop began to rise, and it's now the case that even admirers of Lowell like McClatchy admit that Bishop has been "by far" the more influential of the two. "It's puzzling," writes McClatchy in a 1994 essay about the state of contemporary poetry, "anyone would have guessed that Lowell, the most prodigiously gifted poet of his generation and the most ambitious, would set the standard." Lowell still has many readers (he was, after all, a remarkable poet), but it's no longer surprising to see a well-known poet and critic like Michael Hofmann describing the publication of the two poets' collected correspondence in 2008 as "a further episode in Bishop's increasingly sweeping posthumous triumph over her more obvious, more ambitious, more square-toed friend."

———

Yet there's that word again: "ambition." How can someone like Hofmann, who has little patience for Lowell and great admiration for Bishop, nonetheless describe Lowell as "more ambitious"? And why, if Bishop has indeed achieved a "posthumous triumph," is she still paired with Lowell so frequently? Their intimate friendship can't fully explain it; after all, Gerard Manley Hopkins and Robert Bridges were also close friends who wrote interesting letters to each other, but nobody talks about Hopkins and Bridges as if they were Hall and Oates. So why are Bishop and Lowell any different?

The complete answer to that question involves larger societal issues that are beyond the scope of this book. But the short answer has to do with style: When we talk about poetic ambition, and by extension poetic Greatness, we're talking about style and persona, even when (or maybe, especially when) we think we aren't. We expect "ambition" and "Greatness" to announce themselves in a certain way, and if they don't, we're slow to recognize them. Our assumptions, which are largely unconscious, work like a velvet rope: If a poet looks the way we think a great poet ought to, we let him or her into the club quickly—and sometimes later wish we hadn't. If a poet fails to fit our assumptions, though, we spend a lot more time checking out the poet's outfit, listening to the poet's friends importuning, weighing the evidence, waiting for a twenty, and so forth. Of course, this only matters for poets whose reputations are still at issue. It may have taken Emily Dickinson a hundred years to be considered "ambitious," let alone "Great," but now that she's there, she's there. For contemporaries and near contemporaries, though, falling on the wrong side of our intuitions can mean trouble, because those intuitions give rise to chatter and criticism and scholarship that can take decades to clear away.

What, then, do we assume ambition and Greatness look like? There is no one true answer to that question, no neat test or rule, since unconscious assumptions are by nature unsystematic and occasionally contradictory. Generally speaking, though, the style we have in mind tends to be grand, sober, sweeping—unapologetically authoritative and often overtly rhetorical. It's less likely to involve words like "canary" and "sniffle" and "widget" and more likely to involve words like "nation" and "soul" and "language." And the persona we associate with Greatness is something, you know, exceptional—an aristocrat, a rebel, a statesman, a prodigious intellect, a mad-eyed genius who has drunk from the Fountain of Truth and tasted the Fruit of Knowledge and donned the Beret of . . . Well, anyway, it's somebody who takes himself very seriously and demands that we do so as well. Greatness implies scale, as I mentioned earlier, and a Great poet is therefore a big sensibility writing about big things in a big way. These are the signs we look for first when we're appraising a poet's ambition, and if we find them—or if we think we find them—a particular series of assumptions is set in motion.

————

To get a sense of what I mean, let's look quickly at some representative lines from Lowell and Bishop. There's no way to do either poet perfect justice in an excerpt (particularly Lowell, whose *Collected Poems* is over twelve hundred pages long), but it should be possible to get a feel for the styles at issue. Here is what so-called early Lowell looks like; this is the beginning of "Falling Asleep over the Aeneid," which is about an old man who dreams that he is Aeneas at the funeral of Pallas, an Italian prince:

> The sun is blue and scarlet on my page,
> And *yuck-a, yuck-a, yuck-a, yuck-a,* rage
> The yellowhammers mating. Yellow fire
> Blankets the captives dancing on their pyre,
> And the scorched lictor screams and drops his rod.
> Trojans are singing to their drunken God,
> Ares. Their helmets catch on fire. Their files
> Clank by the body of my comrade—miles
> Of filings! Now the scythe-wheeled chariot rolls
> Before their lances long as vaulting poles . . .

And here is later, looser Lowell; this is the conclusion to his well-known poem "Skunk Hour" (which is dedicated to Bishop):

One dark night,
my Tudor Ford climbed the hill's skull;
I watched for love-cars. Lights turned down,
they lay together, hull to hull,
where the graveyard shelves on the town. . . .
My mind's not right.

A car radio bleats,
"Love, O careless Love. . . ." I hear
my ill-spirit sob in each blood cell,
as if my hand were at its throat. . . .
I myself am hell;
nobody's here—

only skunks, that search
in the moonlight for a bite to eat.
They march on their soles up Main Street:
white stripes, moonstruck eyes' red fire
under the chalk-dry and spar spire
of the Trinitarian Church.

I stand on top
of our back steps and breathe the rich air—
a mother skunk with her column of kittens swills the
     garbage pail.
She jabs her wedge-head in a cup
of sour cream, drops her ostrich tail,
and will not scare.

Poetic style is a complicated thing, to be sure, but it's also in many ways a function of diction. So what kind of word is Lowell drawn to? In the first excerpt, we find "scarlet," "rage," "mating," "fire," "captives," "pyre," "scorched," "helmets," "fire" (again), "lances," and so forth. In the second, we find "dark," "skull," "graveyard," "bleats," "blood," "throat," "hell," "red," "fire," "swills," "garbage," "jabs," and "scare." Exciting stuff, no? There are many other effects that make up the full Lowell style—for instance, the occasional use of hard enjambment ("Yellow fire / Blankets . . .") and widely fluctuating line length—but Lowell's word choice provides a basic, if necessarily incomplete, sense of his approach. That approach, it seems fair to say, involves diction that is conspicuously intense and/or heightened.

Now let's consider a representative sample of Bishop's writing. Here is the conclusion of "Poem," in which Bishop's speaker examines a seventy-year-old family heirloom, a tiny painting possibly meant as a preliminary sketch for a larger effort. As the speaker looks at the small scene depicted in the painting, she realizes:

> . . . Heavens, I recognize the place, I know it!
> It's behind—I can almost remember the farmer's
>   name.
> His barn backed on that meadow. There it is,
> titanium white, one dab. The hint of steeple,
> filaments of brush-hairs, barely there,
> must be the Presbyterian church.

Would that be Miss Gillespie's house?
Those particular geese and cows
are naturally before my time.

A sketch done in an hour, "in one breath,"
once taken from a trunk and handed over.
Would you like this? I'll probably never
have room to hang these things again.
Your Uncle George, no, mine, my Uncle George,
he'd be your great-uncle, left them all with Mother
when he went back to England.
You know, he was quite famous, an R.A. . . .

I never knew him. We both knew this place,
apparently, this literal small backwater,
looked at it long enough to memorize it,
our years apart. How strange. And it's still loved,
or its memory is (it must have changed a lot).
Our visions coincided—"visions" is
too serious a word—our looks, two looks:
art "copying from life" and life itself,
life and the memory of it so compressed
they've turned into each other. Which is which?
Life and the memory of it cramped,
dim, on a piece of Bristol board,
dim, but how live, how touching in detail
—the little that we get for free,
the little of our earthly trust. Not much.

About the size of our abidance
along with theirs: the munching cows,
the iris, crisp and shivering, the water
still standing from spring freshets,
the yet-to-be-dismantled elms, the geese.

What are the most important words in this excerpt? Perhaps the best answer to this question isn't a list of words at all, but rather the curious diffidence with which the poem handles a single key word: "vision." "Our visions coincided," writes Bishop, yet "'visions' is / too serious a word—our looks, two looks." "Poem" is very much about "vision"—artistic vision, the vision of memory, the long vision that comes from the perspective of familial generations—yet Bishop backs away from the one word that fits her poem most closely (and that is also the only word that seems as if it might belong in a Lowell poem). And she does so because it is "too serious."

————

What does Bishop mean by this? Surely not that the poem itself is unserious; after all, like almost all of Bishop's writing, "Poem" takes up very serious subjects indeed. One way to interpret this peculiar refusal might be to say that Bishop wants to be sure we understand that what matters is the ordinariness of the painting and of her speaker's response. She wants us to see that "seriousness" is already a part of even our most casual aesthetic experiences and our most trivial-seeming memories, such that these "small" things can't easily be separated from the "big" stories we tell ourselves about our own lives ("Which is which?" she asks). Bishop is in many ways one of the great American poets of bad art— or at least, of amateurish and primitive art—and the point she's making here about the potential "seriousness" of such work has echoes elsewhere in her own writing, in poems such as "Large Bad Picture" and "The Monument."

But when Bishop declares the word "vision" to be "too serious," she's also making a point about style. She's suggesting that the best way to signal "seriousness" in a poem is not necessarily to use words that are themselves "serious"; in fact, that using such words amounts to a failure of style that resembles a failure of manners—a kind of clumsy explicitness, like announcing, "I am certainly enjoying all of this erotic touching!" in the middle of a sexual encounter. Bishop is asking us instead to find "seriousness" in things that are unstated, indirect, hard to see, and sometimes even hidden ("Life and the memory of it cramped, / dim, on a piece of Bristol board, / dim, but how live . . ."). This is very different from Lowell's style, which stakes its "seriousness" on the representative ability of words like "rage," "mating," "fire," "captives," "pyre," "scorched," "helmets," "dark," "skull," "graveyard," "bleats," "blood." When Lowell writes in "Epilogue" that "*[t]he painter's vision is not a lens, / it trembles to caress the light*," it's no surprise to see that the word "vision" appears unaccompanied by a disclaimer.

It's also not surprising that Lowell's style immediately appealed to readers in the 1960s and 1970s who longed for ambition and Greatness. After all, it looked the way it was supposed to look. And Lowell looked right as well: He was a thunderbolt-chucking wild man from one of America's most famous Bostonian lineages, and his breakdowns, break-ups, and escapades are still talked about in the poetry world the way Marilyn Monroe's drug problems still get occasional ink in *Star* magazine. (One example: Having decided that the poet and critic Allen Tate would be instrumental in his poetic development, the twenty-year-old Lowell showed up at Tate's house expecting to be asked to move in. When told by an amused Tate that the house was, in fact, already full, Lowell pitched a tent in the yard and lived in it for three months.) Bishop, on the other hand, had neither a style that was recognizably ambitious, nor a persona that might substitute for her tendency to begin poems with lines like "In Worcester, Massachusetts, / I went with Aunt Consuelo / to keep her dentist's appointment . . ." Consequently, it's taken thirty years for us to conclude that, yes, it's possible (maybe, perhaps) that Bishop's "modesty" and "charm" might have been concealing ambition—and that the ambition in question was to be Great.

But our assumptions about how Greatness should look, like our assumptions about how people should look, are more subtle and stubborn than we realize. So in certain segments of the poetry world, there is still a tendency to make Bishop what you might call "Great with an asterisk." In particular, as I mentioned before, there has been a persistent effort to pair her with the greater-looking but less-read Lowell, a ploy that resembles the old high school date movie tactic of sending the bookish Plain Jane to the prom with the quarterback (when her glasses are slowly removed by the right man, she's revealed to have been, all along, totally hot!). For example, in reviewing *Words in Air: The Complete Correspondence Between Elizabeth Bishop and Robert Lowell* for *The New York Times Book Review* in 2008, the critic William Logan depicted the two poets as star-crossed lovers despite the fact that (1) Bishop was a lesbian; and (2) Lowell's only romantic overture to Bishop in their thirty-year friendship—and this was a man who would've made a pass at a fire hydrant—was met with polite silence by its intended recipient. Yet while this flight of fancy is almost comically unfair to both writers, it does provide a workable if unwieldy model of ambition and Greatness. Bishop wrote the poems, Lowell acted the part, and if you simply look back and forth fast enough between the two while squinting, it's possible to see a single Great Poet staring back at you.

————

But surely, you may be thinking, this kind of thing doesn't go on anymore. Surely the days are gone when we were at the mercy of what Auden once called "prejudice [that] blinds us to what our real tastes are." Well, yes and no. It's true that we've become much better at recognizing the value of approaches that are indirect or that seem small or silly, and this is largely a byproduct of Bishop's slow ascendancy. But we still have a tendency to associate certain virtues with particular styles, regardless of whether the poet or poem in question actually fits the praise we're offering. In particular, many readers still assume that a poet who is ambitious will have a style that involves abstraction, overt deployment of rhetoric, words that connote bigness, philosophical name-dropping, and so on. If there is to be joking and whimsy, then that joking and whimsy will be of a particular witty, knowing sort; at no point will anyone's foolishness risk actual embarrassment.

So what does such a style look like today? Obviously there are many variations—style is, after all, complicated stuff—but the following poem is reasonably representative:

The storm: I close my eyes and,
standing in it, try to make it *mine*. An inside
thing. Once I was. . . . once, once.
It settles, in my head, the wavering white
sleep, the instances—they stick, accrue,
grip up, connect, they do not melt,
I will not let them melt, they build, cloud and cloud,
I feel myself weak, I feel the thinking muscle-up—
outside, the talk-talk of the birds—outside,
strings and their roots, leaves inside the limbs,
in some spots the skin breaking—

but inside, no more exploding, no more smoldering, no
    more,
inside, a splinter colony, new world, possession
gripping down to form,
wilderness brought deep into my clearing,
out of the ooze of night . . .

....

Let mind be more precious than soul; it will not
Endure. Soul grasps its price, begs its own peace,
Settles with tears and sweat, is possibly
Indestructible. That I can believe.
Though I would scorn the mere instinct of faith,
Expediency of assent, if I dared,
What I dare not is a waste history
Or void rule. Averroes, old heathen,
If only you had been right, if Intellect
Itself were absolute law, sufficient grace,
Our lives could be a myth of captivity
Which we might enter: an unpeopled region
Of ever new-fallen snow, a palace blazing
With perpetual silence as with torches.

....

Where are your monuments, your battles, martyrs?
Where is your tribal memory? Sirs,
in that gray vault. The sea. The sea
has locked them up. The sea is History.

First, there was the heaving oil,
heavy as chaos;
then, like a light at the end of a tunnel,

the lantern of a caravel,
and that was Genesis.
Then there were the packed cries,
the shit, the moaning:

Exodus.
Bone soldered by coral to bone,
mosaics
mantled by the benediction of the shark's shadow,

that was the Ark of the Covenant.

As you may have guessed, the above isn't really a poem at all; rather, it's a pseudo-poem cobbled together with quotes from (in order) Jorie Graham, Geoffrey Hill, and Derek Walcott. The point isn't that these three writers all sound alike—they don't, for the most part—but rather that their work shares some basic assumptions that make a patchwork like the above possible and plausible. Those assumptions can be summarized by a quote Graham gave once in an interview: "I think many poets writing today realize we need to recover a high level of ambition, a rage, if you will—the big hunger." There are those words again: "rage," "big," "hunger." What Graham is talking about here isn't ambition, but style; and what Graham is longing for isn't measurable achievement (for instance, as Frost put it, "to lodge a few poems where they will be hard to get rid of"), but a certain sort of *look*. It's a reasonable thing for a poet to want, but as readers, we should do our best to avoid the mistake of assuming the wardrobe is the measure of the poet.

Yet that's something we still do on a regular basis. The poets mentioned above vary in ability, but when they receive positive reviews, the language of those notices is remarkably . . . similar. As in:

> . . . the urgency and vision of the poems . . . People
> always say about Graham that her poems are big and
> ambitious, that she's a gorgeous writer, and she's
> notoriously "difficult," as a lot of original poets are. Her
> difficulty usually has to do with her magic . . . Graham
> is also notoriously intelligent . . .
>
> —ROBERT HASS, *The Washington Post*, SEPT. 28, 1997

> Hill rapidly shifts from one mode to the next as he
> proceeds through the poem's 150 separate sections
> . . . Always an exquisitely, even excruciatingly self-
> conscious poet, he now turns on himself with fresh
> intensity, interrogating his aims and means even as he
> defends them . . . Hill's work has always been difficult,
> a resistantly private art weighted with literary allusion

. . . There is no climax to its agonized mental action, no definite promise of relief.

—LANGDON HAMMER, *The New York Times Book Review*,
JAN. 17, 1999

. . . Derek Walcott's [poetry] represents something akin to a resounding evolutionary leap . . . [W]riting with an orphic sonority and bardic bravura seldom heard in Anglophone poetry since Dylan Thomas or Yeats . . . [H]ighlights the formal prowess of the progressively ambitious work he's produced over the last 20 years . . . [T]aken as a kind of symphonic overture to an as-yet-unfinished canon of prodigious scope and gravity, it . . . confirm[s] the incantatory powers of an oracle the likes of which the New World hasn't seen since Prospero drowned his book.

—DAVID BARBER, *The Boston Globe*, FEB. 25, 2007

Notice the terms of praise: "intelligent," "difficult," "agonized," "intensity," "big," "symphonic"—these are, as I've argued, exactly the kind of words we associate with ambition and Greatness. Of course, one might say that this kind of description makes perfect sense, because all three of these poets are indeed ambitious and Great. It's hard to argue with this response, even if it does bring to mind the story of the orchestra conductor who, after passing over fifteen female violinists for the string section, finally chose a man, remarking, "At last! A player with ambition!" But the real question isn't why critics have found the qualities described above in Graham, Hill, and Walcott; rather, the question is why critics *don't* resort to this kind of vocabulary when considering widely admired writers whose styles are notably different.

Consider, for example, Kay Ryan. Ryan has had a very successful career by any measure—she was the Poet Laureate from 2008 to 2010 and won the Pulitzer Prize in 2011. Even if she hasn't won the Nobel (like Walcott) and doesn't hold a fancy chair at Harvard (like Graham, who got the Pulitzer fifteen years before Ryan, despite being five years younger), and even if she doesn't often get called "the greatest living poet in the English language" (like Hill), Ryan is nonetheless an indisputably esteemed writer. But that admiration often takes a distinctively curious form. Here, for example, is how David Kirby described her work in a *New York Times* review from 2005:

> There is a brash, exuberant poetry being written
> in America these days, a long-lined, many-paged,
> pyrotechnic verse . . . This isn't it. A Kay Ryan poem
> is maybe an inch wide, rarely wanders onto a second
> page, and works in one or two muted colors at most.

Kirby likes her work, however, so that less-than-enthused opening rapidly gives way to praise:

> Ryan's are the biggest little poems going . . . So Kay
> Ryan's tiny poems turn out to be full of color and

argument, after all. In fact, she makes good writing
look so easy that I despair of her influence . . .

Now, this is positive any way you look at it. But it's worth
noting the approach that even a critic who likes Ryan's work
feels obligated to take. That approach consists of two steps:
(1) acknowledging that the poems in question are "small";
and (2) explaining why they are nonetheless worthwhile—
and perhaps even "big."

Why, if Ryan's poems are actually "full of color and argu-
ment," is this oddly backward method necessary? To answer
that question, it's necessary to have some idea of what a Kay
Ryan poem looks like. Here is "Outsider Art":

Most of it's too dreary
or too cherry red.
If it's a chair, it's
covered with things
the savior said
or should have said—
dense admonishments
in nail polish
too small to be read.
If it's a picture,
the frame is either
burnt matches glued together
or a regular frame painted over

to extend the picture. There never
seems to be a surface equal
to the needs of these people.
Their purpose wraps
around the backs of things
and under arms;
they gouge and hatch
and glue on charms
till likable materials—
apple crates and canning funnels—
lose their rural ease. We are not
pleased the way we thought
we would be pleased.

As you can see, Ryan's style is very different from Graham's or Hill's. She relies on "modest" diction ("apple crates," "nail polish"); her phrasing is casual, if sometimes convoluted ("Most of it's too dreary"); and her habit of concluding poems in a snappy, aphoristic manner makes it unlikely that anyone would ever call her work "difficult" (even if, in many ways, it is). In other words, Ryan does exactly the opposite of what we expect an "ambitious" poet to do. As a result, if we find ourselves admiring Ryan's work and sensing *something* (ambition, perhaps?) that makes it worth returning to, we assume that we have to explain our response in a way that we do not, for instance, feel we need to explain a similar response to Hill's writing. Hill looks the part; Ryan doesn't. And as I've tried to suggest, our assumptions about the way writers should look are far more deeply seated than we realize.

———

But where do those assumptions come from? Partly they come from the nature of the words we're using in evaluation. "Ambition" and "Greatness" make us think of grandness and scope, so in our less subtle moments we look for lines that exhibit those qualities in an overt way. Yet our literary assumptions aren't just a matter of how we perceive different styles; they're also shaped by the reputation-making structures of the poetry world. We'll never be able to read all the poems in the world, nor could we possibly take in all the critical comments made about those poems. So what we see is determined by what poets, critics, and readers have said and done in the past—and also by the systems that were created (or that evolved) to handle the task of deciding who gets to say what about whom. As you might expect, changes in those structures can have peculiar effects on our thinking.

Here, it's useful to have a little institutional history. For most of the twentieth century, the poetry world resembled, well, a country club. One had to know the right people; one had to study with the right mentors. The system began to change after the GI Bill was introduced (making a university-level poetic education possible for more people), and that change accelerated in the 1970s, as creative writing programs began to flourish. In 1975, there were eighty such programs; by 1992, there were more than five hundred, and the accumulated weight of all these credentialed poets began to put increasing pressure on poetry's old system of personal relationships and behind-the-scenes logrolling. It would be a mistake to call today's poetry world a transparent democracy (that whirring you hear is the sound of logs busily rolling away), but it's more democratic than it used to be—and far more middle class. It's more of a guild now than a country club. This change has brought with it certain virtues, like greater friendliness and courtesy. One could argue that it also made the poetry world more receptive to writers like Bishop, whose style is less ponderous and hoity-toity than, say, Eliot's. But the poetry world has also acquired new vices, most notably a tedious careerism that encourages poets to publish early and often (the Donald Hall essay I mentioned some pages ago is largely a criticism of this very tendency). Consequently, it's not hard to feel nostalgic for the way things used to be; or at least, the way we imagine they used to be. And this nostalgia often manifests as a preference for a particular kind of "ambition" and "Greatness."

Indeed, it's regularly assumed that these two qualities are somehow missing from poetry, and that this is the result of a loss of nerve that occurred in the late 1930s—which is, not coincidentally, the time at which the first American creative writing program was founded. For instance, the critic James Longenbach, in response to Graham's comment about "the big hunger," argues that "[she] is right to suggest that a kind of expansiveness, a certain rhetoric of ambition, became difficult for poets after modernism." This does not, in fact, appear to be the case—around the middle of the century, Robert Lowell and the bombastic Dylan Thomas were two of the most famous poets in the English-speaking world—but it's revealing that even a reader as reliably perceptive and intelligent as Longenbach believes Graham's statement to be basically reasonable. We see in the Noble Elsewhere the ambition that seems so sadly lacking in the ordinary here and now.

———

One of the easiest ways to see this phenomenon in action is to look at a peculiar development in American poetry that has more or less paralleled the growth of creative writing programs: the lionization of poets from other countries, especially countries in which writers might have the opportunity to be, as it were, shot. In most ways, of course, this is an admirable development that puts the lie to talk about American provincialism. In other ways, though, it can be a bit cringeworthy. Consider the way in which Robert Pinsky describes the laughter of the Polish émigré and Nobel-winning dissident Czesław Miłosz: "The sound of it was infectious, but more precisely it was commanding. His laughter had the counter-authority of human intelligence, triumphing over the petty-minded authority of a regime." That's one hell of a chuckle. The problem isn't that Pinsky likes and admires Miłosz; it's that he can't hear a Polish poet snortle without having fantasies about barricades and firing squads. He's by no means alone in that. Many of us in the American poetry world have a habit of exalting foreign writers while turning them into cartoons. And we do so because their very foreignness implies a distance—a potentially "great" distance—that we no longer have from our own writers, most of whom make regular appearances on the reading circuit and have publicly available office phones.

In addition, non-American writers are the perfect surface upon which to project our desire for the style and persona we associate with old-fashioned ambition and Greatness. One hesitates to invoke the dread word "colonialism" here, but sometimes you've got to call a *Mayflower* a *Mayflower*. How else, really, to explain the reverse condescension that allows us to applaud pompous nonsense in the work of a Polish poet that would be rightly skewered if it came from an American? Miłosz wrote many fine poems, to be sure, but he is also regularly congratulated for lines like:

What is poetry which does not save
Nations or people?
A connivance with official lies,

A song of drunkards whose throat will be cut in a
    moment,
Readings for sophomore girls.

Any sophomore girl worth her copy of *A Room of One's
Own* would kick him in the shins.

———

It may be starting to sound as if "ambition" and "Great-
ness" are simply euphemisms concealing predictable preju-
dices that poets should forswear on their path to becoming
wise and tolerant twenty-first-century artists. That is,
however, almost the opposite of the truth. Yes, Greatness
narrowly defined to mean a particular, windily dull type of
writing is something we could all do without, and long may
its advocates gag on their pipe smoke and languish in their
tweeds. But the idea that poets should aspire to produce
work "exquisite in its kind," as Samuel Johnson once put it,
is one of the art form's most powerful legacies.

How is that aspiration embodied today? The answer, as I
hope you've seen, is that we don't know. There is no "true"
way to be ambitious, just as there's no "proper" way to write
poetry; instead, we exist in a flurry of possibilities that will
bring to mind either snowflakes or bullets, depending on
your disposition. We invent, we borrow, and we do our best.
That process is, in part, what Devin Johnston has in mind in
his short lyric "Mockingbird":

We live each other's death
and die each other's life,
borrowing a cold flame
from sycamore in early leaf.
This morning, after heavy rain

the street erupts with birds:
grackles sharpen swords
and cedar waxwings strip
the vines, declaring love and war.
With tail cocked, I guard the stoop

from strangers, ill at ease.
As sunlight strikes a wheel,
I think as Sulla thought—
hostis, host and enemy
to any sound that swells my throat.

Like Sulla, the first Roman general to march on his own
city, the mockingbird holds a power that is both its own and
not its own: the many songs it sings, all of which come from
the birds it guards against. If we think of this in terms of
style—and in a poem, birds are always poet stand-ins—
then what "Mockingbird" suggests is that the styles through
which a poet speaks are both his strength (because he is the
one using them) and his weakness (because they're by na-
ture derivative). The best thing he can do is hold to what he

knows—his stoop—and keep his position among the vast and cacophonous surge of styles, against which his own music can so easily be lost. But if he's lucky and determined, he survives the surrounding racket and produces something that is, if not new, at least difficult to forget. And that hope, when it becomes a conviction, is what it means for a poet to be *ambitious*.

the fishbowl

YOU CAN LEARN A good bit about poetry by paying attention to what poets do when they aren't writing. That may at first seem like a strange claim; after all, we don't assume that hanging around in a math department faculty lounge will give us insights into things like $u_t = 6uu_x - u_{xxx}$; nor do we imagine that snooping on a bunch of off-duty surgeons will tell us how to remove a spleen. So if we want to understand poetry, shouldn't we be focusing on the still, small voices of poems themselves, and not let ourselves be distracted by whatever huffing and puffing the literary crowd does in its downtime?

Well, not exactly; or rather, not entirely. Poetry is written by humans, not angels or elves, and the humans who write poetry tend to be interested in the same thing that humans who write PowerPoint presentations are interested in: doing well for themselves, and perhaps just a bit better than their colleagues. And poetry itself can never be proved right or wrong, effective or ineffective, beneficial or harmful; it can only be agreed to be interesting, which means that those very human humans are constantly in the business of persuading themselves and everyone else to pay attention. This is why the literary universe has always resembled a sales department office toward the end of the month (or a high school cafeteria around prom time), despite the perception among some readers that the essence of writing involves disinterested solitude atop cloud-wreathed peaks. "History," said Oscar Wilde, "is merely gossip"—and while that's not precisely true of poetry, it does seem fair to say that understanding the art form means having at least some notion of the chatty, schmoozy, often desperate reality its contemporary practitioners inhabit.

One might argue that this is a cynical way to look at poetry and poets. But there are good reasons to pay attention to what goes on behind the scenes in Poetryland, and most of those reasons have little to do with cynicism and everything to do with the practical realities involved in writing and reading literature. Chief among these is the simple fact that, as Elizabeth Bishop observed, we can learn a great deal about the way a poet relates to the world by looking at "his or her life, and letters, and so on" in addition to his poems. Understanding poetry means understanding a way of thinking, and concepts explored in poems are often also a part of tossed-off emails, notebook scribbles, and barroom conversations. That said, it's important to remember that the point of learning more about poets' lives is to learn more about poets' poetry, not to do the equivalent of snickering in the supermarket line over whatever *Us Weekly* is saying about the latest follies of Courtney Love. Although in fairness, this can be fun, especially when we're talking about Ezra Pound, who was sort of the Courtney Love of his day.

Another reason chatter and gossip are worth paying attention to is more a matter of sympathy: It's hard to be a poet. It's true, of course, that poetry will never cause a broken bone (at least, not directly), nor do poets run the risk of being shot (unless they are very, very bad). But poets face two obstacles that in combination are nearly unique in American society. First, most people have no idea what they do. This means that they must struggle to earn a living, and that any existence they achieve either will be achingly lonely or will be buttressed by the company of other poets, which in itself could be considered a form of loneliness. Second, even if most people don't know what poets do, the average person feels that whatever it is, it must be *spectacular*. This is in part because our culture has a long history of treating poetry as a metaphor for excellence, suitable even for activities that have nothing to do with writing. (Sportscasters regularly describe plays as "pure poetry"; references to "pure choral singing" are harder to come by.) But poetry is rarely spectacular to those who haven't spent much time with it, and only occasionally spectacular even to those who have. So poets are constantly confronted not only with widespread ignorance about their art, but with the fact that anything they write will inevitably disappoint an audience conditioned to associate poetry with sublimity. Given these difficulties, it seems only fair to explore the ways in which poets think about their own day-to-day lives—if only so that we can better appreciate the angst that lies behind those slim and glossy volumes in Barnes & Noble.

———

The average American poet spends much of his time sending dozens of envelopes filled with poems to literary magazines read by, at most, a few hundred people. Most of these magazines are supported by universities, and most of those universities have creative writing programs, and most of those creative writing programs are stocked with as many poets—at both the student and faculty levels—as can manage to squeeze themselves in. This wasn't always the case. In the first half of the twentieth century, poets like T. S. Eliot, Wallace Stevens, William Carlos Williams, and Marianne Moore wrote poetry while working in jobs that were thoroughly unpoetic. Williams, for instance, was a doctor, while Stevens had perhaps the least romantic occupation ever conceived by a Western society: insurance company executive. Other writers supported their art with family fortunes ranging from the ample (Gertrude Stein, Hart Crane) to the barely adequate (Robert Frost).

But as I mentioned in the previous chapter, things started to change in the first few decades of the twentieth century. Partly inspired by the example of Robert Frost, who joined the Amherst faculty in 1917, poets began to enter the academy as lecturers and artists-in-residence, and soon other colleges followed the University of Iowa (which established its Writers Workshop in 1936) in offering graduate programs in creative writing. The rise of the creative writing industry has had a number of consequences for American poetry, but the one that interests us here is simple: It changed the way poets relate to each other and to their work. What had previously been an occupation composed of loners and occasionally interlocking coteries became—well, not exactly a profession, but what the sociologist Ailsa Craig has smartly called "an *illusion of profession*." Poets began giving readings on a circuit of sorts (as Auden puts it in "On the Circuit": "God bless the lot of them, although / I don't remember which was which: / God bless the U.S.A., so large, / So friendly, and so rich"). They began to worry even more, if possible, over whether their writing was au courant. They began to hold *conferences*.

These developments have not gone unnoticed or unprotested. As recently as 2006, John Barr, the president of the Poetry Foundation, complained that "an academic life removes [poets] yet further from a general audience," and writers like August Kleinzahler still take regular shots at the idea of the professional academic-poet ("What to make of them, the professors / in their little cars, / the sensitive men paunchy with drink / parked at the fence / where the field begins and the suburb ends?"). Of course, the poets making these accusations have come in for their share of grief too—David Fenza, the head of the Association of Writers & Writing Programs, accused Barr of "a very peculiar kind of myopia or amnesia" and Kleinzahler has more enemies than Zorro. There's a pleasing amount of absurdity to be found on both sides of these arguments, which emerge on a roughly five-year cycle like overeager cicadas. But the more important point is this: The poetry world has changed, and it's likely to remain in its current configuration for the foreseeable future. And that configuration affects the way poets view themselves and each other both inside and outside their poetry.

———

This is not, contrary to what's often argued in pieces about the imminent death of poetry, an entirely regrettable development. After all, any art is always colored by the circumstances of the artists who make it, and the university positions held by most poets have a great deal to recommend them. As scholars like Robert Crawford have pointed out, there is a rich historical relationship between poetry and academia that stretches back at least as far as the Enlightenment. That connection today allows a good number of poets to have regular paychecks and health insurance, which in turn has allowed many more people (and types of people) to participate in the art form. This is an unambiguously good thing, despite the grumbling it has sometimes provoked from poetry's snobbier precincts. In addition, poets have demonstrated that not only can they function on a campus, they can occasionally get some reasonably good material out of one. Here, for instance, is Thom Gunn being louche in "Office Hours":

> these big handsome
> sweaty boys
> with their goatees
> and skateboards
>
> these sharp chic
> ironic girls
> with brisk hairstyles
> and subtle tattoos
>
> we sit close
> but sexuality
> is grandly deferred
> because the ground
> on which we meet
> is Bunting's flexible
> unrepetitive line
> or Wyatt's careful
> sidestepping of danger . . .

And here's the start of Billy Collins's best poem, which focuses on the wildly unpromising subject of writing workshops and is called, appropriately enough, "Workshop":

> I might as well begin by saying how much I like the
>   title.
> It gets me right away because I'm in a workshop now
> so immediately the poem has my attention,
> like the Ancient Mariner grabbing me by the sleeve.
>
> And I like the first couple of stanzas,
> the way they establish this mode of self-pointing
> that runs through the whole poem
> and tells us that words are food thrown down
> on the ground for other words to eat.
> I can almost taste the tail of the snake
> in its own mouth,
> if you know what I mean.
>
> But what I'm not sure about is the voice,
> which sounds in places very casual, very blue jeans,
> but other times seems standoffish,
> professorial in the worst sense of the word . . .

Is this the great work of our age? Probably not. But it's pleasurable writing, and certainly no worse than what we'd have if poets all worked in splendid isolation punctuated only by yelling matches and the occasional affair. However we may romanticize it, the poetry world of the past was often a cliquish mess, and we're surely better off under today's regime.

———

That said, the current structure does have its weak spots, and many of them result from friction between poetry's present, quasi-academic status and the art form's other, decidedly nonacademic legacies. As Mark McGurl observes in *The Program Era: Postwar Fiction and the Rise of Creative Writing*, this friction is inevitable and to an extent intentional: "[I]t is precisely an unresolved tension between the 'confinement' of institutionality and the 'freedom' of creativity that gives creative writing instruction its raison d'être as an *institutionalization of anti-institutionality*." Poetry fits into the academy, then, by not entirely fitting in. In order to understand how this complicated dynamic works in practice, it's useful to think of the modern poet as a kind of hybrid creature, like a centaur. There are two obvious ways for a centaur to get itself into trouble: It can forget that it's part horse (in which case sitting at a restaurant table is going to be awkward), or it can forget that it's part human (in which case grazing isn't going to turn out well). Similarly, poetry can find itself caught between two mistaken assumptions about its role— on the one hand, that it's just another academic discipline, and on the other, that its relationship to the university is nothing more than a matter of practical convenience. Since these two misconceptions lead to very distinct sorts of problems, let's look quickly at each of them individually.

The clearest indication that poetry is now sometimes regarded as "just another academic discipline" is that the benchmarks of academic success are frequently, if unconsciously, adopted by some readers as a measure of achievement in a particular writer's career *as a poet*. This is indirectly evident in the general and relatively recent tendency to regard "the book" as professional documentation, a standard by which several significant poets of the nineteenth and twentieth centuries would have fallen short. But it's also easy to find critical writing in which it's assumed more or less explicitly that poetry's primary duty is to the university system. In 1997, for instance, the critic Marjorie Perloff, a professor at Stanford, devoted a nine-thousand-word essay to complaining that poetry reviewing in general-interest publications is done by "minor poets or . . . professional reporters" as opposed to "a poetry specialist (e.g., an English professor)." She was especially unhappy that one of her favorite groups of writers had been curtly dismissed in a review, a response that she viewed as untenable because the poets in question had inspired "so many articles, books, and symposia." Indeed, one of the books "has appeared on course syllabi across the U.S. . . . , has become a popular item on PhD qualifying exams, and is cited . . . with increasing frequency." Some of its ideas had even been "discussed in learned journals." Finally:

> My own sense is that [a] middle-class poetry public no
> longer exists, that poetics is now at least as specialized
> as is architectural discourse; indeed, the latter actually
> speaks to a much wider audience than does poetry,
> given that everyone lives and works in specific
> buildings and hence takes an interest in the look and
> feel of the built environment. In the case of poetry,
> however, the rapprochement with the university may
> well be a *fait accompli*.

This kind of thinking puts poetry in an unfortunate position for many reasons, and one of the most telling is sadly practical. If McGurl is correct that a creative writing program's vitality depends on it being both of and not of the university system, then an art that seems wholly absorbed by that system is in danger of losing its appeal. Indeed, if a poet's success may be measured in "articles, books, and symposia," as well as being "cited . . . with increasing frequency," then it's hard to see why anyone should write poetry at all. Why not write controversial scholarly articles instead? After all, those *really* snare citations. The difficulty with treating poetry as if it were a subsidiary of the academy isn't so much that doing so risks turning poets into English professors, but that it risks turning them into second-rate English professors.

But another, equally troubling set of problems can arise when the responsibility that poets owe to the university system is underestimated. Precisely this sort of underestimation was at the root of American poetry's first true scandal of the digital age, which is generally known as "the Foetry episode" or "that awful Foetry site" or "oh, God, the Foetry thing—have you seen it?" In short: Foetry.com was a website run anonymously with the stated purpose of "exposing the fraudulent 'contests.' Tracking the sycophants. Naming names"—by which the site's regulars meant revealing the web of personal connections that resulted in poetry competitions that were, in their view, essentially fraudulent. This was a serious accusation, because competitions are the way in which many, if not most, books of poems are published nowadays. For example, when you see a phrase like "Winner of the Colorado Prize for Poetry" on the cover of a collection, it means that the manuscript in question was selected in an open competition to be published by the Center for Literary Publishing in conjunction with the University Press of Colorado, which is run by Colorado State University. Typically, books published through these competitions have a series editor who appoints judges each year, and in some cases those judges are anonymous. In addition, these contests cost money to enter—usually around thirty dollars or so.

You can see how this might be a problem. Every year, large numbers of poets, many of them already having paid thousands of dollars for MFA degrees, end up spending hundreds more for the chance to publish a book (a necessity for academic employment) in competitions judged anonymously, generally by older poets with many former students, friends, lovers, and so forth—in other words, people with debts to pay and legacies to protect. It's an almost head-on collision between poetry's coterie tendencies and its academic responsibilities, and consequently a recipe for, if not disaster, at least a lot of quiet loathing and barely suppressed fury.

And that was exactly what one found on Foetry. The site was stocked with outraged allegations of favor-trading, creepy insinuations about people's personal lives, and buckets of name-calling (including my personal favorite, "foet," which referred to careerist poets). But beyond its entertainment value, there were two things that were remarkable about the site's brief run from 2003 to mid-2007. The first was that people outside the poetry universe paid attention— the Foetry site inspired more than a dozen articles across the country in publications from *The Boston Globe* to the *Los Angeles Times*. Second, the site actually managed to document some of the more egregious ethical lapses in the contest system. As the *San Francisco Chronicle* put it:

> [S]ome of Foetry's examples appear to show true
> conflicts of interest—such as the case of the University
> of Georgia Press' Contemporary Poet Series. As in
> many contests, the judges had not been named. Cordle
> [Alan Cordle, the research librarian eventually outed
> as Foetry's administrator] secured documents through

a public-records petition last year, revealed their
identities dating back to 1979, then documented the
connections between judges and winners. Confirming
what many suspected, judges frequently awarded poets
with whom they had personal relationships. Among
the poet-judges implicated were Pulitzer Prize–winner
Jorie Graham at Harvard University; MacArthur fellow
C. D. Wright at Brown University; and former U.S.
poet laureate Mark Strand at the University of Chicago.

And there you have it. While the behavior at issue here is
plainly unacceptable, it's important to remember that poetry's
history is largely built around small gangs of like-minded art-
ists and peculiar, close, charged friendships. In such arrange-
ments, the idea of fair play doesn't typically extend to people
outside the group. Nor is that attitude necessarily to be criti-
cized: If you and your friends are struggling to get attention, it
hardly makes sense to spend each brief moment in the spotlight
talking about the gang down the street. (Think of it this way:
We might roll our eyes because Francis Ford Coppola cast his
own daughter, Sofia Coppola, as Michael Corleone's daughter
in *Godfather III*, but we don't think of that act as being *wrong* in
the way that, for instance, embezzlement is wrong.) So what
Foetry documented was, in many ways, just poets being poets.

But most poets aren't "just poets" anymore. They're also
attached to the academy, which means that they have respon-
sibilities to the general public, as well as to the thousands
of people paying for MFA degrees. And while the academic

world is not a place in which favor-trading and glad-handing are unknown, there is at least a sense among professors that such things are supposed to be dignified, or at any rate not obvious. There is a sense, however imperfectly realized, that the work is supposed to do most of the talking, and that one should be careful about allowing personal feeling or private benefit to influence professional judgment. Yes, academia often falls well short of these standards, but they remain standards in the sense that one can be reproached for violating them. What Foetry revealed was that poets could—and would—be reproached for violating them as well, at least when the activity at issue reflects directly on the university system. As the majority of poetry publishing does.

———

All of which leaves poets in an awkward spot. On one hand, they're confronted with the standards of fairness and civic responsibility that exist for professors; on the other hand, they're drawn (and expected to be drawn) to the art form's rambunctious, impassioned history of oddball behavior and outrageous self-promotion. (Whitman, for instance, wrote anonymous reviews of his own book in which he described himself as "[o]ne of the roughs, large, proud, affectionate, eating, drinking, and breeding, his costume manly and free, his face sunburnt and bearded . . .") And while a poet's life may revolve around the university, he's much less likely to achieve tenure, and hence a measure of stability, than a normal academic. Consequently, poets inhabit an unstable, in-between position in almost every way: professionally, economically, artistically. Does the centaur belong with men or with horses? It's hard to be sure.

This uncertainty matters. Perhaps more than anything else, it matters because it limits poets' ability to talk plainly and confidently about what they do—it's difficult, after all, to communicate when you're not sure whom you're speaking to, or for. As a result, public conversations about poetry can have a strangely excessive, erratic quality. Poets regularly engage in mutual adoration that would embarrass a roomful of swingers, yet it's equally easy to find examples of rage-filled frustration that will put you in mind of Buffalo Bills' fans on the morning of January 31, 1994.

To give you a better sense of how volatile the talk about poetry can get, let's return quickly to the example of Foetry. Any site taking up the cause of people who feel they've been unjustly mistreated or ignored, and which furthermore allows those people to complain anonymously, is obviously not going to be an exercise in politesse. But there's anger and then there's Foetry. As more than one critic noted at the time, the tone of the site often went well beyond legitimate outrage and deep into the territory of bug-eyed crazy. Consider the following representative quotes:

[C]an I go on record as saying you suck cock? I know some people like to suck cock, but I am saying you can suck mine, after I go for a four-mile jog.

[I]f you are [name omitted] you are a snitch who sold
out your fellow poets, just like the cowards of the 50's
sold out their friends during the McCarthy hearings.

And of course:

Look asshole, you know nothing about me . . . you
might think you've done so much for poetry but what
yr doing is shit you little fucker . . . I bust my ass,
kill myself everyday for this shit . . . and have for ten
fucking years . . . seven of which I've spent teaching
you fucking turd . . . and I never had any fucking
secret gang at [omitted] so fuck yr pal too . . . your
stupid fucking website is a pile of crap and so so so
much wasted energy . . . like this email, but fuck you
again . . . you had BETTER HOPE I NEVER SEE
YOU IN PERSON YOU FUCK!!!! AND NO I don't
have to respectably engage with you as you're the
one who initiated the fucking insulting discourse you
shit . . .

Not exactly what you think of when you think "poets in
conversation," is it?

And yet, as I've said, this rage is balanced by a species
of sycophancy that can be equally appalling. This is best
demonstrated by poetry's own unique blurb culture, which
over the past forty years has grown ever more exquisitely ri-

diculous, like a rosebush on steroids. To get the full effect of
the modern poetry blurb, it's best to work up to it slowly, so
let's begin by considering a couple of blurbs on very differ-
ent sorts of books. The first appears on the back of *The State
of Speech* by Joy Connolly, a classics professor at NYU, and
was written by Robert Kaster at Princeton:

> This is an admirable book in every way: in its ambition
> to read Roman rhetorical thought seriously, as political
> thought, in the breadth of its reference and the depth
> of its learning, and in its desire to connect the mores of
> the Roman Empire with our own.

A clean, straightforward, professional plug—unambigu-
ous but far from slobbery. Next, here's Louise Erdrich's
blurb on the cover of David Treuer's novel *Little*:

> An exciting find, complex and compelling. David
> Treuer has written an ambitious novel of extraordinary
> emotional range.

Again, a pretty uncomplicated recommendation. But now
consider the poet Cole Swensen's blurb for *A Point Is That
Which Has No Part*, a collection from 2000 by Liz Waldner:

> Liz Waldner asserts. Several things: "Language is a
> solid," and/or "We're being turned into information

(read: language)." It begins with names. And should we try to stop it? Waldner is not running the usual social critiques—not even the bright, incisive ones—she's pushing on into a zone where the ambiguity breaches morality. But very subtly. This is not a place to sleep. And while you're being uneased awake, you'll also be entertained. If language is a body, it's certainly very sexy, and maybe if we can sufficiently appreciate the high wire act, we won't be turned into electronic blips.

This paragraph is many things, but uncomplicated isn't one of them. Yet in its knotty combination of pseudo-academic speak ("a zone where the ambiguity breaches morality") and effusive weirdness ("If language is a body, it's certainly very sexy"), Swensen's blurb isn't out of the ordinary—or at least, not *that* out of the ordinary—for a contemporary poetry endorsement. If you're having trouble believing that, try this sentence from Julie Sheehan's blurb for *Mortal Geography* by Alexandra Teague, which I just received in the mail while writing this paragraph:

Read *Mortal Geography* line by plumb line, so you can hear it hit with bliss-stoked erudition its every adventure, prayer, address to the dead and near, blood-soaked episode from history's hand-written transcripts, and ruined praise: there's a hum, a thunking heartwood, then a quiver.

As with the disproportionate anger to be found on the Foetry forums, this rhetorical extremity is related to poetry's uncertain status. When you're not entirely sure what you are, it's easy to believe you're everything (and therefore deserving of all possible praise) or nothing (and therefore deserving of the bleakest scorn). And so the contemporary poet sits uneasily in a place of unease, a mixed creature longing for purity.

———

But what, you may be wondering, does any of this have to do with poetry as it exists on the page? Aren't blurbing and ranting and contests and existential angst ultimately just a sideshow? The short answer is, not exactly. The slightly longer answer is that these structural and psychological features affect poetry in ways both direct and indirect, and while it generally will be impossible to trace the causation behind the technical aspects of any given poem—"This line break is *clearly* the result of the poet's residency at Yaddo!"—that doesn't mean that the poem exists in a vacuum. Much as the growth of trees is affected by the quality of the soil, the writing we call poetry is affected by the methods we've developed to produce, distribute, and discuss it.

In many ways, this is obvious. Consider, for instance, publishing and reviewing. The structure of the poetry world helps determine which books end up in print, which in turn determines what poems audiences have the opportunity to hear about and read, which in turn determines what the average, educated person believes to be "poetry," which in turn has an effect on how many poets feel about their own work. Eventually technological developments may change that dynamic, but as of 2011, it remains very much the case that publishing a book is essential to being considered a poet, and that getting attention for that book is essential to being considered an Important Poet. If you want an academic job, you can't wait until you're forty, as Robert Frost did, before getting your work between covers. So today we're getting more poems more quickly from more people, many of whom are hoping for the same type of employment, and almost all of whom have no audience outside the art form itself. It's hard to say this turn of events doesn't affect our experience of poetry, however much we may like to believe that the poet composes in solitude, accompanied only by the ghostly whispers of his mighty forebears.

Fortunately, most of the editors and judges involved in poetry publishing are good people doing admirable work, often for very little obvious reward, so much of their influence is mild and possibly even beneficial. Still, as the Foetry episode helps demonstrate, behavior that has very little to do with poetry can nonetheless determine not only which books make it onto shelves, but which collections actually get discussed. One short and typical example from my own arena: An enterprising poet-critic failed to turn in a review for a well-known publication of a younger poet's first book.

The editors checked in with the critic a few times over several weeks, but received no response. Months later, they discovered that the reviewer had not only gotten in touch with the poet, told the poet about his assignment, and claimed to have written a rave—but that he had then blamed the editors for the failure of this alleged rave to appear in print. (The editors, as the reviewer likely knew, are constrained by a number of ethical, practical, and business reasons from explaining any of this to the unfortunate writer.) Why would anyone behave like this? Who knows? But that's one less book of poems a reader might see covered in the publication in question.

———

When thinking about these issues, it can be helpful to imagine the poetry world as a kind of restaurant. One sits down, one orders a poem, one waits for deliciousness to ensue. But how we end up feeling about our meal can be a function of many things—the memory of the waiter (we'll never know what an appetizer tastes like if he forgets to bring it out), the dexterity of a busboy, even the opinions of the restaurant critics (how we respond to a given dish is, after all, partly a function of how we expect to respond to it). The experience of reading poetry, no less than the experience of eating, is a complex blend of memory and sensation, anticipation and argument: It's about the food, but it isn't *only* about the food.

And of course, even the food isn't just about the food. Which is to say that the sort of extrapoetic factors I've been discussing appear explicitly and repeatedly in the words of poems themselves; they are a part of what makes poems poems. That's because poets, like all authors, write about what they know—and one of the things they know best is the existence they share with other poets. If changes in the poetry world have changed the way that poets relate to one another, then we should see that emerge, however obliquely, in the actual lines that poets write. Of course, sometimes the emergence is anything but oblique, as in Thom Gunn's epigram "To Another Poet":

> You scratch my back, I like your taste it's true,
> But, Mister, I won't do the same for you,
> Though you have asked me twice. I have taste too.

Yes, it's a poem premised on blurb solicitation. Gunn's wry, pointed take is unusual in some respects, because it's addressed directly to another writer and is mocking rather than complimentary (although Gunn doesn't tell us who's managed to annoy him). Indeed, satirical poems aimed at other poets aren't common these days, probably because so much of a poet's career depends on, if not gaining the goodwill of other poets, at least managing to avoid their active enmity. Dryden may have written of Thomas Shadwell that he "stands confirm'd in full stupidity," and for that matter, Jay-Z may have told Nas, "I've got money stacks bigger than you," but the typical lyric involving contemporary poets is more like Rachel Zucker's "Poem":

The other day Matt Rohrer said,
the next time you feel yourself going dark
in a poem, just don't, and see what happens.

That was when Matt, Deborah Landau,
Catherine Barnett, and I were chatting,
on our way to somewhere and something else.

In her office, a few minutes earlier, Deborah
had asked, are you happy?

Sounds pretty friendly—and that isn't meant to be a
criticism of Zucker or her peers; there are, after all, plenty
of things more interesting than watching poets insult each
other. But it's interesting to see professional collegiality crop
up in the lines of an art that historically has been, for better
or worse, distinctly lacking in that quality.

Yet if poets typically aren't mocking one another by name
in poems, or complaining, or otherwise heaving pots and
pans, that doesn't mean they're reluctant to address some of
the stickier issues I've been discussing. Consider Mark Hal-
liday's "Loaded Inflections":

. . . At lunch

Brian praises Geffle's new book and I say, "Well, but
it all seems so humorless" and a little later

I praise Conkley's recent book and Brian says, "Maybe
but the poems seem so cozy, so pleased to whip up
the same yelp of the Tortured Spirit, over and over."

Next day having coffee with Eric
I rather recklessly praise some of Prinshod's poems
and Eric says, "If only he wasn't always
mounting his bardic steed"
and we both laugh at how apt this criticism indeed is.

And later in the same poem:

. . . although
we're not stupid enough not to know
that in another café in Boston or Madison or New
    Haven
or Ann Arbor or Baltimore or Houston
or Iowa City or Manhattan or Berkeley
someone who has published three "well-received"
    books
is commenting very briefly
on my new book, or Eric's, saying of Eric
"he pretends to know much more than he knows," or
"he never sounds like a real person" or saying of me
"Halliday thinks his most banal experiences are poetry
    already" . . .

This poem couldn't exist without the particular confluence of gossip and art that characterizes American poetry today (and it shouldn't surprise you that Halliday also has written a poem about tenure). That's not to say that "Loaded Inflections" lacks antecedents: Its jaunty, ironic take on literary politics can be traced back at least as far as Catullus, who claimed that the book of one of his rivals, Volusius, "will remainder in Italy, / a cheap & all too abundant wrapping for mackerel." Yet where Catullus is direct and confrontational—Volusius was a real person— Halliday isn't interested in naming names and settling scores (no, there's no poet called Prinshod). Consequently, his poem isn't about literary politics so much as how poets feel about literary politics, and how they hope (or fear) that poetry itself transcends literary politics. As a piece of writing, it exists at one remove.

Which brings us, finally, to perhaps the most curious example of the ways in which poems can reflect the realities of the contemporary poetry universe. You may recall from high school the dreaded "poem about poetry," of which William Carlos Williams's "The Red Wheelbarrow" is perhaps the most fearsome example. Modern technology has improved on that device. We now have what you might call "the poem about how the poet feels about the way poets think about poetry, as related to other poets." Typically these poems traffic in romantic notions of purity and are delivered in a high-minded tone that's reminiscent of the Otter defense in *Animal House*, minus the irony. Take, for example, this section from Jennifer Moxley's "The March Notebook":

What the new brand cannot understand
effectively becomes unreadable,
slightly feared and somewhat baffling,
even a charity case. Who attempts to have
a view we eventually will undo. Suddenly
they will find themselves waking up
on the wrong side of everything, their heroes
being carted off to prison. And we feel good,
don't we, when turning the lock of judgment
on yet another broken life, exulting as we exit
the dungeon, tossing the key into a field
of unkempt, matted earth. This is the moment
we have ceased to feel the breathing of others
beneath our feet. The question must be stifled:
How many lives do we cast aside because they ask
too much of us? They threaten the simple pride
we take in everything we write . . .

Moxley is talking here about how we read certain poets poorly or not at all, based on our own aesthetic needs as poets, and how this behavior is, in a larger sense, unfair, because it ignores the sacrifice these writers have made, and woe, alas, alackaday. All of these are fair observations, only . . . what if "we" aren't poets? Or what if we *are* poets, but just not poets who think it's remarkable that writers are sometimes unfair to one another? What if we think that this particular injustice ranks significantly below jaywalking, and maybe one tick above bogarting the nachos?

The point here is not that Moxley is a poor writer—on the contrary, she's a talented and often graceful one. The point is that a poem like this makes sense only in the context of the contemporary poetry world and is intended to be read solely by poets who see themselves as invested in that world's various dilemmas. Lawyers don't have fits of angst over discarding legal doctrine that's no longer useful, even though that doctrine was almost certainly someone's life's work. Doctors don't worry over whether it's fair to use new technology. Philosophers don't use purple phrases like "broken life" and "carted off to prison" to describe disputes over the semantics of counterfactuals. But as the poetry community has become more and more insular, changes in style have become increasingly important—because for many poets, there's no life beyond the familiar circle of inward-facing faces. When one is out of fashion, it can indeed feel almost like being abandoned. So Moxley is writing about a subject that's of real concern for poets; the problem is that it is of concern only for poets. In reviewing the 2003 movie *Shattered Glass*, which told the story of a real-life plagiarism scandal at *The New Republic*, Anthony Lane wondered, "If the internal turmoils of a political magazine based in Washington are now considered sufficient grounds for a motion picture, there is no saying where the movie industry, avid for fresh material, will choose to cast its net: a struggle for the soul of *Men's Health*?" By the same token, we might say here: If the familial bickering of the poetry world is now considered sufficient grounds for a poem, what's next—a sequence about how upset one is at having been left off a panel at the AWP conference? Behind the expressions of concern and compassion in a poem like "The March Notebook" lies the assumption that failing to read poetry judiciously is a moral failing.

———

Still, it may be something akin to this overvaluing that allows poets, every now and then, to find within their own gossip the gossip of the larger world. In order to speak, after all, one needs a position to speak from. As I've suggested, there is a lingering sense among poetry readers that literary politics and other sociological features of a poet's existence are somehow separate from—and implicitly, of lesser stature than—the serious business of writing poetry. Often, this judgment is framed as a kind of finger-wagging: "Shouldn't you be ashamed to be talking about [insert gossip], when we should really be talking about Poems?" And we are all duly shamed, because of course it's very hard to write poems, and

they can be very serious indeed, and most poets are sensi-
tive, obsessive people who believe in their art and want to
do right by it.

But this isn't quite fair. There is no shame in acknowl-
edging the social universe that we inhabit, because only by
doing so can we hope to have any perspective on that reality.
Such perspective allows us not to "transcend" the various
absurdities of the poetry world, but rather to write appropri-
ately and confidently from within them. In "The Old Poet,
Dying," August Kleinzahler recounts a bedside vigil for a
friend; the poem begins:

> He looks eerily young,
> what's left of him,
> purged, somehow, back into boyhood.
> It is difficult not to watch
> the movie on TV at the foot of his bed,
> 40" color screen,
> a jailhouse dolly psychodrama:
> truncheons and dirty shower scenes.
> I recognize one of the actresses,
> now a famous lesbian,
> clearly an early B-movie role.
> The black nurse says, "Oh dear"
> during the beatings.
> — *TV in this town is crap*, he says.

Kleinzahler goes on to describe his friend's wandering conversation as he drifts in and out of consciousness ("He is telling a story. / Two, actually . . . The river in Oxford— / he can't remember the name . . ."). The poem concludes:

> *— Have you met what's-his-name yet?*
> he says.
>> *You know who I mean,*
> *The big shot.*
>>> *— Yes*, I tell him, *I have.*
> *— You know that poem of his?*
> *everyone knows that poem*
> *where he's sitting indoors by the fire*
> *and it's snowing outside*
> *and he suddenly feels a snowflake*
> *on his wrist?*
> He pauses and begins to nod off.
> I remember the name of the river
> he was after, the Cherwell,
> with its naked dons, The Parson's Pleasure.
> There's a fiercesome catfight
> on the TV, with blondie catching hell
> from the chicana.
> He comes around again and turns to me,
> leaning close,
>> *— Well, of course*, he says,
> taking my hand,

his eyes narrowing with malice and delight:
— That's not going to be just any old snowflake,
now, is it?

So even in his final moments, a poet takes time to get in a dig at the self-regard of a rival (who is, in case you're wondering, the poet Mark Strand, whose 1998 collection, *Blizzard of One*, contains the snowflake in question). This is a poem about death, of course, and the sadness we all feel at the diminishment of a companion. But it's also a poem about the specific life a poet leads, in which complaining about narcissists and "big shots" is as natural as taking breath. Nor can "The Old Poet, Dying" tell us about the former without accepting the latter. The triviality and pettiness of the old poet's "malice and delight"—which Kleinzahler quietly matches with the venom of a B-movie prison scene—are precisely what allow the poem to become something more than a simple story about triviality and pettiness. However briefly, the malice becomes truth, and the delight becomes beauty. And each snowflake is indeed special, no less so for living within the blizzard.

middle of the BCS championship game in order to announce to the room at large, "Yes, the battle between the Alabama D-line and the Texas O-line is compelling thus far, but is this really the best way for us to spend three and a half hours?" You do, however, find poets engaging in soul-searching, navel-gazing, and defensive rationale-proffering on a more or less regular basis. This behavior has an extensive history, which can be roughly summed up by noting that two of the most famous essays ever written about poetry are titled "A Defence of Poetry" (by Percy Bysshe Shelley) and "An Apologie for Poetrie" (by Sir Philip Sidney).

It's easy to get caught up in the peculiarities of this anxiety. Are its roots, for instance, mostly a matter of bad luck? If we'd had different poets at different times, might contemporary poetry have managed to gain a sense of cultural and existential security comparable to that of pop music, or at least NASCAR racing? If political or technological changes had occurred more slowly or quickly, could that have altered the way we look at poems? Or is there just something intrinsic to poetry that causes the art form to exist in a state of perpetual self-doubt? These are, or can be, interesting things to think about. But speculation like this can also be a way to avoid what is, after all, a straightforward question: Why should anyone spend time reading or writing poems when that person could be doing something else, like learning about electrical engineering or watching an episode of *Top Chef*? Why, in short, should we bother with poetry—as it exists today, right now—at all?

There are two primary ways to think about this question. The first is to put on our philosopher hats (or beards) and embark upon an examination of the nature of value and choice, being sure to cover the finer points of Aristotle, Kant, Mill, Wolf, and rational choice theory. Fortunately, this isn't a book about philosophy, so we can leave the contemplation of these not-exactly-poetic subjects to the people who get paid to worry about them. The second, less technical way of thinking about why we read poetry is simply to look at the reasons most frequently offered by people who work with the stuff on a daily basis. Why do poets, critics, and poetry readers think poems are worth bothering with? What special claims do they believe can be made on poetry's behalf? If we want to learn why something is worth doing, this seems a practical way to go about it.

———

Before going any further, though, I should make a confession: I don't think most of the claims made for poetry are especially helpful. So when I say that we should investigate those claims, I mean that we should try to understand the ways in which they're confused, inflated, or simply wrong. Poetry comes to us tricked-out in centuries of overheated rhetoric; for example, consider a typical remark made by Shelley in the essay mentioned previously: "As to his glory, let time be challenged to declare whether the fame of any other institutor of human life be comparable to that of a poet." It's useful to cut away the more absurd bits of costuming surrounding poems, if only to reassure ourselves that real flesh still lies beneath the embroidery.

So let's begin with the most basic problem with the typical defenses of poetry: Many of them underestimate the issue being confronted. In particular, the typical defense of poetry tends to assume that it's enough to point out that the art form does something interesting or clever or attractive, when the real difficulty lies in demonstrating that poetry does something so interesting, clever, or attractive that people should forego other activities in order to enjoy its interestingly clever attractiveness. This is a quandary that capital-L Literature and its defenders find hard to avoid. In his essay "Why Read the Classics?" for instance, Italo Calvino spends nearly all of his space trying to figure out what a "classic" is in the first place, only to conclude: "The only reason one can possibly adduce is that to read the classics is better than not to read the classics." That sounds modest enough. But in fact, Calvino misstates the dilemma, because no one chooses between reading the classics and not reading the classics where "not reading the classics" means something like "sitting around and staring blankly into space." No, people choose between reading the classics and making soup, or going to the zoo, or studying physics, or ministering to the sick, or any of a thousand other activities that directly benefit the world, or humanity, or themselves. And if this presents a dilemma for "the classics," it's an even more uncomfortable question for contemporary poetry, which is by definition not yet "classic" itself, and often not even very good at all.

Granted, this may seem like an unnecessarily rigid way of looking at human existence. We don't like to think of our lives as a series of grim moral confrontations that require us constantly to ask questions like "If I take ten minutes to play Dice Wars online, have I wrongly deprived the world of ten minutes I might have spent researching charities for orphans?" Life would be bleak indeed without frivolity, to say nothing of Dice Wars. But poetry isn't truly frivolous in this sense, because learning to read it well takes considerable effort and significant time (especially since few of us grow up with it as part of our daily lives). Sure, ten minutes to play an Internet game is nothing to worry over—but how about the thousand hours it takes to get a basic familiarity with modern poetry and its extraordinarily long tradition? If we exclude early childhood, the average person has approximately three hundred thousand hours of waking life. Can we say with confidence that a thousand of those hours should be devoted to an obscure art form whose entire national audience could be seated in a typical college football stadium with room to spare? Are we so sure of what poems have to offer?

———

Some people certainly seem to be. It's impossible to list all the unique claims made on poetry's behalf, but they can be loosely grouped under three overarching assertions:

1. Poetry has a special connection to language, or is itself a special sort of language, or does something special *to* language, or at any rate, has something to do with specialness and language.
2. Poetry has a unique connection with our *selves*. It tells us who we are, where we're going, where we came from, etc.
3. Poetry has a special position relative to society and/or culture. It "bears witness" or "preserves traditions" or "resists ideologies," depending on who's wanting it to do what, and where that person sits on the political spectrum.

These are vague categories, to be sure, but they do represent the sorts of things that get said about poets and poetry. And there's some truth to each of them. But the question, again, is not, "Does poetry have qualities that are interesting and/or worthwhile?"; rather, the question is, "Are poetry's interesting and worthwhile qualities sufficient to displace the interesting and worthwhile qualities of another activity?" For these claims to be meaningful, then, they need to describe qualities either that are *only* demonstrated by poetry, or that poetry possesses to such a degree that other activities make unappealing substitutes. With this in mind, let's take a slightly more detailed look at each of these assertions.

First, of course, there's the matter of poetry and language. Possibly you recall being told in a long-ago English class that language itself is only "fossil poetry" (Emerson); maybe you remember hearing that poetry is supposed to be "the best words in the best order" (Coleridge); perhaps you've even run across the contention that poetry is "the universal language which the heart holds with nature and itself" (Hazlitt). To pick a more recent quotation, you may have happened upon Pulitzer Prize winner and former poet laureate Rita Dove's declaration that "[p]oetry is language at its most distilled and most powerful." All of these assertions represent what we might call the "Poetry as Super Language" school of thinking, and as you can see, that school inclines toward the not exactly modest. Indeed, whenever a contemporary poet starts talking like this—and there are plenty of examples—the conversation often becomes increasingly grandiloquent, as if the poet in question has just finished watching the extended edition of *The Fellowship of the Ring* and is now imagining himself striding like Gandalf across some vast subterranean space, preparing to wield that sacred fire, Poetry, against a profoundly unlucky Balrog.

This excessiveness obscures an insecurity, or at least an uncertainty. Because the more one thinks about these claims, the more unlikely it seems that poetry has a unique association with "language." Language, after all, is big. At any given moment, over a billion people are speaking or writing in English—do we imagine that nearly all these billion people are failing to achieve the coruscating majesty attained by contemporary poets? Do we think that in their silences, interruptions, declarations, and outbursts, these people don't manage effects that equal or even surpass the richness of contemporary poems? When a parent says, "I love you" to his or her child, and that child realizes, for the first time, what those words actually mean, do we suppose that poetry—*any* poetry—could equal the transformative impact of that understanding? A sculptor works with substances that his audience may never have touched; a musician plays an instrument that his listeners have never mastered. But a poet uses the same words that hundreds of millions of people use every day to marry, fight, console themselves, entertain, grieve, and order cheeseburgers. It seems bold at best to argue that all of these people have somehow failed to "get" the intricacies of language in the way that a few thousand poets do, much as it would seem bold for an ant clinging to your shoelace to announce, "Look at me steering this enormous creature!"

Along the same lines, it's hard to see how poetry does something in or to or with language that isn't managed just as effectively by some other activity. Take, for instance, Dove's assertion above that poetry is uniquely "distilled" and "powerful." Ask yourself which of the following seems to be the most distilled:

Admittedly I err by undertaking
This in its present form. The baldest prose
Reportage was called for, that would reach
The widest public in the shortest time.
Time, it had transpired, was of the essence.
Time, the very attar of the Rose,
Was running out. We, though, were ancient foes,
I and the deadline. Also my subject matter
Gave me pause—so intimate, so novel.
Better after all to do it as a novel?

—OPENING LINES OF *The Book of Ephraim*

BY JAMES MERRILL

Just do it.

—NIKE COMMERCIAL

Merrill's poetry is distinguished in many ways, but "distilled" isn't a word that rushes to mind. As for the suggestion that poetry is especially "powerful," consider these two quotations:

In a red winter hat blue
eyes smiling
just the head and shoulders

crowded on the canvas
arms folded one
big ear the right showing

the face slightly tilted
a heavy wool coat
with broad buttons

gathered at the neck reveals
a bulbous nose
but the eyes red-rimmed

from over-use he must have
driven them hard
but the delicate wrists

show him to have been a
man unused to
manual labor unshaved his

blond beard half trimmed
no time for any-
thing but his painting

—"SELF PORTRAIT" BY WILLIAM CARLOS WILLIAMS,
FROM *Pictures from Brueghel*, WINNER OF THE
PULITZER PRIZE FOR POETRY IN 1963

. . . I am cognizant of the interrelatedness of all
communities and states. I cannot sit idly by in
Atlanta and not be concerned about what happens in
Birmingham. Injustice anywhere is a threat to justice

everywhere. We are caught in an inescapable network of mutuality, tied in a single garment of destiny. Whatever affects one directly, affects all indirectly. Never again can we afford to live with the narrow, provincial "outside agitator" idea. Anyone who lives inside the United States can never be considered an outsider anywhere within its bounds.

—FROM "LETTER FROM BIRMINGHAM JAIL"

BY MARTIN LUTHER KING JR., 1963

There's much to admire about William Carlos Williams, but King's text is more "powerful" in at least two senses. First, when we talk about writing having power, we usually mean that the writing in question is rhetorically rich. King's passage is filled with memorable phrasing ("a single garment of destiny") and vivid parallelisms ("Whatever affects one directly, affects all indirectly"); Williams's lines are as plain as can be (which is deliberate, of course). Second, the real-world effect of King's "Letter"—and what is power without consequence?—was and is greater than probably any American poem yet written.

Again, this is not to say that poetry isn't interesting or moving or clever or even, in its own way, powerful. It's frequently all of those things. But it isn't the *only* verbal activity that meets those descriptions, nor is it necessarily the one that meets them best. The closer we look at the unique claims made for poetry and "language," the more we realize that in order to defend those claims, we're going to be forced to adopt one of two untenable positions. We can either (a) ignore the fact that poetry plays almost no role in the language of most people; or (b) expand the definition of poetry so as to make the art form meaningless (for instance, we can claim that all fictional and/or figurative language is a subset of poetry, which is like asserting that all games played with vaguely spherical objects are really ping-pong). What we can't do, unfortunately, is offer a straightforward argument for poetry along the lines of "Only through poetry can we understand X about language," where X is something uniquely desirable. The best we can do is to say that only through poetry can we understand poetry.

———————

Which may not be such a bad thing. Before we talk about why that might be, though, let's quickly dispense with the other two assertions that get made regularly about poetry. These are, as I've said, the idea that poetry has a special connection to our selves and the notion that poetry has a special connection to society and culture. I've already discussed these ideas in "The Personal" and "The Political," respectively, so let's focus here simply on what keeps each notion from providing a clear-cut rationale for reading or writing poetry.

The basic problem with declaring that poetry is associated in some unique way with our innermost selves is obvious: The overwhelming majority of English-speaking humanity knows nothing whatsoever about poetry, yet many of those people seem to lead inner lives that are perfectly satisfactory. So we can either assume that these seemingly contented people are deluded, and doomed to a soulless oblivion of which they're sadly unaware, or we can acknowledge that whatever one gets from poetry must also be obtainable from other sources.

Similarly, the difficulty with assigning poetry a special role in culture or society is that poetry currently plays only a modest role in either by any reasonable measure. We might, of course, attempt to turn this apparent handicap into an advantage by arguing that poetry's irrelevance serves as a kind of subtle social critique—that poets, by remaining almost completely unknown and without any noticeable influence on anything whatsoever, have successfully resisted the reification of "art" for placid consumers by refusing to participate in the capitalist system of commodification and creating communities of unalienated workers who . . . Anyway, whatever one thinks of this sort of argument, the problem is that it doesn't do much to answer the question "Why read poetry?" Because even if we assume that poetry's insignificance is actually a sly form of significance, it still leaves us with no good answer for the person who asks, "Well, if insignificance to the larger culture is a virtue, why shouldn't I do something just as insignificant as poetry but infinitely more fun, like joining the Coney Island Polar Bear Club or collecting interesting bits of bark?" The only thing we can do in response to this kind of question is shrug. And maybe point toward some promising birch trees.

Now, of course, would be a good time to reverse field and acknowledge all the flaws in the preceding paragraphs. To admit, for example, that almost no activity can withstand the question "Why do this, when I might be doing that?" To suggest that poetry's benefits aren't measurable in the way that the benefits of medicine or engineering are measurable. To say that our aesthetic responses are complicated, and that poetry's long and often proud history makes it especially suited to engage those responses, even though the art form may manage that feat for only a small number of people, or after many decades have passed. To argue, along similar lines, that the sheer persistence of poetry over so many hundreds of years and in the face of so many competitors should discourage us from dismissing it. To point out that rhetoric about poetry isn't meant to be taken *literally*.

But I'm not going to say any of these things, because I really do believe that poetry is hard to recommend. Further, I believe that it's hard to recommend in a way that many other activities aren't. Yes, it's possible to poke holes in whatever answers we might come up with to questions like "Why be a firefighter?" or "Why watch movies?" or "Why pay attention to American politics?" But it's much easier to undermine the claims made for modern poetry—and this, perhaps, should tell us something. Nor is it much of an argument to say that these claims aren't meant to be taken seriously. If declarations about poetry's various virtues aren't serious, at least in some way, then there's no point in making them in the first place.

So what are we left with? Perhaps nothing more than the realization that much of life is devoted to things that in the end don't matter very much, except to us. Time passes whether we like it or not, and its too-quick progress is measured out in private longings and solitary trivialities as much as in choices we might defend to a skeptical audience. This isn't to say there aren't reasons for us to love the things we love—Robert Frost was wrong, or at least not entirely right, to say that we "love the things we love for what they are." But those reasons can be difficult to describe in the way that it's hard to describe what red looks like, or how one's relationship with a child or parent feels. The same is true of poetry. I can't tell you why you should bother to read poems, or to write them; I can only say that if you do choose to give your attention to poetry, as against all the other things you might turn to instead, that choice can be meaningful. There's little grandeur in this, maybe, but out of such small, unnecessary devotions is the abundance of our lives sometimes made evident.

———

It's only mildly inaccurate to say that before I went to college, I knew nothing about poetry. Until that point, my poetic education consisted mostly of whatever the public schools of South Carolina could manage, and despite the best efforts of our teachers, that wasn't much. We were "exposed," as curriculum guides put it, to a few Shakespeare plays and a handful of canonical poems like Donne's "The Flea," which went over fairly well, and William Carlos Williams's "The Red Wheelbarrow," which did not. ("So much depends," as one of my classmates put it, "upon this poem sucking.") In my senior year of high school, I was invited to an on-campus scholarship competition at a nearby university in which I was asked to write an essay about choices, or decisions, or something along those lines. When I mentioned the essay topic to my host, a junior at the college, he said, "Oh, you could talk about Prufrock." To which I responded, "Is he a professor here?"

That story is, in its gist if not its details, a relatively common one among poets nowadays. As I've mentioned before, the poetry world began to attract readers and writers from the middle and lower classes in increasing numbers around the middle of the century, partly as a result of the GI Bill. And since the South tends to lag at least one generation behind the rest of the country in educational matters, it's not at all uncommon for middle-class Southern families only now to be producing children who have the opportunity to realize that there is something called modern poetry, and that it might be worth looking at. Myths about the bardic peasantry notwithstanding, poems just weren't something our parents and grandparents had time for. In my family's case, this was certainly true:

My father was, in John Edwards's famous formulation, "the son of a mill worker"—actually one of six sons of a mill worker—and my mother's father was a fireman. All of my parents' planning involved getting my father through law school, in the hope that he would then be able to support the family (which he eventually could and did). My mother has been a devoted fiction reader all of her life, but since she didn't go to college herself, she never had much chance to become familiar with poetry. My father, though relentlessly and sometimes annoyingly intelligent, used to claim that he had owned only one book in his life: *Gridiron Grit*. I never believed such a book actually existed until finally, while writing this chapter, I looked it up online. It's true. *Gridiron Grit* was written by Noel Sainsbury Jr. in 1937 and you can get a copy for $13.80 in "Very Good/Good" condition, taking into account the "small chew on spine hinge."

So like most people, I grew up thinking of poetry as something to be endured in school with the polite determination we typically reserve for tuba recitals and conversations with very old people. For the first year and a half of college that remained more or less the case. In the second semester of my sophomore year, however, I bought Philip Larkin's *The Whitsun Weddings* as part of one of those English Department survey courses in which two hundred years of literature—poetry, fiction, plays, you name it—are condensed into twelve weeks. The book was actually meant for another section, as things turned out. But because *The Whitsun Weddings* is so slim (only forty-five pages from cover to cover) I didn't notice it on my shelf and consequently never returned it to the campus book-store. Months later, looking for something to read, I ran across it and . . . it would be an exaggeration to say my world was instantly changed. But I became interested in poetry in a way I hadn't been interested before. Here's the first poem I remember reading; it's called "Water":

> If I were called in
> To construct a religion
> I should make use of water.
>
> Going to church
> Would entail a fording
> To dry, different clothes;
>
> My liturgy would employ
> Images of sousing,
> A furious devout drench,
>
> And I should raise in the east
> A glass of water
> Where any-angled light
> Would congregate endlessly.

I was struck at the time by two things: Larkin's deliber-ately offhand tone ("If I were called in . . . ," "sousing"),

which was practically the opposite of what I'd thought po-
etry was supposed to sound like; and the contrasting flourish
of the phrase "any-angled light / Would congregate end-
lessly." That dichotomy is characteristic of Larkin, I'd soon
discover, as is the understated wit that sustains and com-
plicates it. For while "Water" is straightforward, it's any-
thing but simple: We know what the poet is talking about;
we just can't be sure how he feels about his subject. Is he, I
wondered, making a joke about belief? After all, the almost
flippant opening, "If I were called in / To construct a reli-
gion," makes the idea of a religious "calling" seem like being
asked to fix the office printer. Or is this a poem about long-
ing to believe? Or to belong? If belief ultimately involves a
congregation of "light" (and not people), then why is the
poem so relentlessly approachable? Why is a poet so inter-
ested in symbols of inhuman purity also determined to talk
to, well, me? And beyond these questions, of course, there
was that phrase: "Any-angled light / Would congregate
endlessly." "Any-angled light" doesn't actually make much
sense, I thought, but at the same time it made perfect sense. It
sounded right. To read it, to say it, made me think (as Larkin
himself once put it), "That's marvelous, how is it done, could
I do it?"

So I read the rest of Larkin's books. Then I read books
about Larkin. Then I read poets who'd been important to
Larkin, some of whom became important to me, and in the
way that an overexcited toddler is guaranteed, no matter how

erratic his progress, to eventually cover every inch of your kitchen floor, I acquired enough knowledge about poetry to feel that I ought to be telling people how (not) to write it. By my second year of law school, I'd published my first review in *Poetry* magazine, and thin collections of poems dominated the likes of Farnsworth's *Contracts* on my shelves. The poet Edward Hirsch wrote an introductory book called *How to Read a Poem and Fall in Love with Poetry* back in the early 1990s, and one gathers from the purplish language that Hirsch uses to describe the art form that he isn't kidding about this "fall in love" business. Had I, then, fallen in love with poetry? Well, we were certainly living together.

———

Here it's worth pausing to note that modern poetry has a peculiar relationship with love, or at least with "love." By this, I don't mean that poetry relates to romance or sex in odd ways (although, thank goodness, it does). No, what I mean is that people who read poetry have a tendency not simply to say that they "like" it or "enjoy" the art form, but rather that they "love" it. And they appear to do this far more than people who are interested in other, comparable things. For example, below is a comparison of the number of results that Google returns when various activities and art forms are plugged into two different searches: "I like X" and "I love X" (for ease of reading, I've listed the relevant ratios, rather than raw numbers):

edly over several days), I never got a result in which "I love poetry" failed to outperform the "like" version; in fact, one particular, presumably aberrant search returned thirty-six occurrences of "love" for every occurrence of "like."

This pattern, conjectural as it may be, fits in with something essential about poetry as it exists today. "A poem," Auden tells us, "might be called a pseudo-person." This is, in one sense, obviously ridiculous; yet in another, more important sense Auden's claim contains an element of truth, because people often view poetry as an activity with which one has a relationship, as opposed to viewing it as something one simply "does." The reasons for this are complex, and likely have to do with a certain kind of rhetoric that became common in the late eighteenth century, as well as with the historical intertwining of poetry with religion (faith is, of course, almost never talked about as something that is "done," but rather "explored" or "reaffirmed"). But regardless of its origins, this way of thinking leads directly to talking about poetry as being an appropriate object for "love." The philosopher Niko Kolodny has argued that love "consists in the belief that some relationship renders it appropriate"—in other words, that we love a person because we stand in a particular relation to that person, and have a particular history (this is opposed to the view that we love people for their intrinsic qualities, or for reasons that are ineffable). We might extend this argument to say that poems, because they're so often viewed as personlike, encourage us to view the long study required to read them as "a relationship," rather than plain old long study. Love, then, becomes a perfectly reasonable next step.

This way of thinking may seem a bit odd, but professions of exactly this kind of "love" are, as Google indicates, relatively common among poets and poetry readers. ("I love poetry," says former poet laureate Mark Strand, "I love myself, but I think I love poetry as much as I love myself.") Talking about poetry in this way has both good and bad effects. On one hand, it encourages a certain sort of poet-critic to declare that various things are "good for poetry" in the self-satisfied tone with which certain couples tell you they're doing something especially annoying—going to yoga together, visiting a therapist, learning to fart in synch—because it is "good for the relationship." On the other hand, there's something lovely, if sad, in the bestowal of such a gift on an activity that not only can never return the sentiment, but lacks even the consciousness to understand the giver's generosity. It seems beautifully pointless, or pointlessly beautiful, depending on your level of optimism.

———

My father died of cancer in March of 2007, as I was beginning work on this book. He was sixty-one. It's difficult to type those sentences for many reasons, not least among them the fact that I've been a book critic for over a decade now, and almost always find myself cringing during the inevitable fetch-me-a-tissue moment in any personal essay or memoir. Still, throughout this book, and especially in this chapter, I've tried to suggest what a relationship with poetry actually looks like, in both its limitations and strengths. I've described it as a private pleasure and an occasional irritation that can't easily be justified in public terms. Having said this, I'd be falling short if I didn't try to offer some sense of what—for me—poetry has proven it can and cannot give. Sad as it may be, we often discover the true contours of any relationship in the situations that matter most to us; and sadder still, those situations tend to be ones in which something we love is lost, or in danger of being lost. So pull out your tissues, and let's talk about that.

Cancer can kill you in many ways, but in my father's case, it was a year-long process of accelerating infirmity. At first, there were only relatively endurable, though far from minor problems—leg pain, sickness from chemotherapy—but about half a year after his initial diagnosis, Dad had his first cancer-related health catastrophe: a stroke. More specifically, he'd had a right hemisphere ischemic stroke, which meant that the left side of his body had lost a great deal of mobility and was, in some places, entirely paralyzed. It also meant that his ability to talk, while not eliminated completely, became warped by what's sometimes known as "flat affect." He would say something like "Look out, you're about to sit on a thumbtack" in exactly the way you'd say "I enjoy knitting doilies in the sunroom." And he had lost much of his ability to indicate pacing and stress differences among syllables, so the previous sentence would actually sound something like "lookoutyou'reabouttositonathumbtack."

The hospital's speech therapist gave us various exercises to try with Dad, many of which revolved around getting him to slow down and modulate his voice. When he was allowed to come home, he soon began working on regaining what he'd lost with the furious persistence he'd always brought to any task but yard work. I moved back in with my parents briefly to help with the rehab, and after several days of witnessing my father's frustration with "lookoutyou're abouttositonathumbtack," it occurred to me—poetry! Of course! What better way to get someone to relearn intonation than to use an art form filled with conspicuous stress patterns? And rhyming! And emotion! Just think of the poignant aptness of the scene: A man who knew nothing about poetry learns to pronounce words again with the help of his son, a poet and critic. It's a vision that, as soon as you have it, quickly mutates into a golden-toned, Oscar-nominated movie directed by Ron Howard and starring a doe-eyed Ethan Hawke alongside a bruised but indefatigable Tommy Lee Jones.

If it seems that I'm being skeptical of my own motives, that's because I am. Like most writers, I've rarely done anything without watching myself doing it, and in this instance, I'm quite sure that I knew I was creating material. But it doesn't matter. My father was hurt; I wanted to help.

Had I been a gardener, I'm sure I would have been trying to find something useful to do with potting soil. Plus, in order for the scenario to be properly cinematic, Dad and I really would need to have been estranged for years, with him disapproving of my flighty ways while I scorned his practicality, until finally we were united under the golden dome of Art as the sun pierced the clouds, etc. But we'd always admired and enjoyed each other, and we'd become closer, not further apart, as I became more involved with poetry. I think, aside from his genuine, generous interest in what I was doing, he relished the thought that his son managed to annoy professors at Harvard. He'd had a rich and full life filled with success, but he was in many ways still a poor mill kid with a chip on his shoulder. Perhaps that helps explain the success.

In any case, flush with inspiration, I searched the house for my leftover college books and returned to Dad armed with the fruits of English poesy. Here is something I learned very quickly: Do not attempt to get a stroke victim to read Hopkins. "I caught this morning morning's minion, king- / dom of daylight's dauphin, dapple-dawn-drawn Falcon . . ." I can barely pronounce that myself, and I have full use of my tongue. We did a little better with Robert Frost. Frost is one of my totem poets, not because he's approachable, but because he is, as Louise Glück once put it, "demonically manipulative." No American poet has better understood the snares and sinkholes of our way of talking. And Frost is also, of course, practically the only poet you can be sure the average person is familiar with—as Dad indeed was. We read "The Silken Tent," which begins:

> She is as in a field a silken tent
> At midday when the sunny summer breeze
> Has dried the dew and all its ropes relent,
> So that in guys it gently sways at ease . . .

It's a brilliant, complicated poem for many reasons, but I've always admired two things in particular: the understated technical virtuosity (the entire poem is a single grammatical sentence), and the delicate exactness of the first line. "She *is as in* a field a silken tent," rather than, for instance, "She *is like* a silken tent in a field." The point here, as the critic Robert Pack puts it, is that "the metaphor of the tent does not merely describe the 'she' of the poem, but rather the relationship between the speaker and the woman observed." "The Silken Tent" therefore gives us a relation (a metaphor) about a relation, which is a more unusual and difficult effect for a poet to attempt than you might suppose.

None of this, mind you, meant much to Dad. For him, the interesting thing about the poem was the tent itself, which, as he reminded us, resembled the tents that were pitched by traveling circuses when he was a boy. True and interesting as this was, and glad as it made me to see him enjoying himself a little, there was something in this response that left me feeling slightly deflated on behalf of my art form. For if reminiscence was all that was needed, we could just as easily have been reading a magazine article about P. T. Barnum. Wasn't there something in the *sound* of the poem that should've been coming through? The syntax? The expert maneuvering that Frost does in order to unload the poem's only four-syllable word in the poem's penultimate line: "In the *capriciousness* of summer air"—couldn't Dad hear that? Shouldn't it help somehow? I had this feeling only for a moment or two, because there were other, vastly more important things to worry about, but it has nonetheless stayed with me for four years. I don't think I'll ever forget it.

———

Because what that feeling told me was that even I, the sensible critic, thought of poetry as a force—for good, for healing, for something—that should be able to lend its vigor even to the uninitiated. But that's not what poetry is. Poetry is a small, vulnerable human activity no better or more powerful than thousands of other small, vulnerable human activities. And poetry, even more than many of these other activities, needs a history with its readers. It needs to have been read, and thought about, and excessively praised, and excessively scorned, and quoted in melodramatic fashion, and misremembered at dinner parties. It needs, in a particular and occasionally ridiculous way, to have been loved. If poetry could do nothing for my father that a thousand other things couldn't do, that was because it hadn't been a part of his life—just as when I'm eventually laid low, I will take little comfort in cello concertos or origami.

And yet it would be inaccurate to say that my father never responded to poetry in the way that Edward Hirsch might have wished. When he did so, however, it wasn't because of some rarity unearthed by the expertise of his clever son, or because of the uncanny genius of one of the definitive poems of our language. No, my mother, probably understanding better than I did the situation Dad was in, went to the bookstore and bought an illustrated version of Edward Lear's classic nonsense poem "The Owl and the Pussycat," which memorably opens:

> The Owl and the Pussycat went to sea
>> In a beautiful pea green boat,
> They took some honey, and plenty of money,
>> Wrapped up in a five pound note.

To say this delighted my father would be putting it mildly. I don't know whether his familiarity with the poem arose from some dim memory from his own childhood, or whether he'd read a similar book to me or my sister when we were kids, but I heard about "the pea green boat" for at least three weeks. We would sit there, my mother, Dad, and I (and my sister when she could—she was in the late stages of pregnancy), and work our way over and over through the land where the Bong-tree grows, near the wood where the Piggy-wig stood. It was happy silliness, soon to end—and surely there were a hundred other things that might have given my father the same comfort—but this absurd poem was, in its own small way, *something*. Here is the end of "The Owl and the Pussycat":

"Dear pig, are you willing to sell for one shilling
    Your ring?" Said the Piggy, "I will."
So they took it away, and were married next day
    By the Turkey who lives on the hill.
They dined on mince, and slices of quince,
Which they ate with a runcible spoon;
And hand in hand, on the edge of the sand,
    They danced by the light of the moon,
        The moon,
        The moon,
They danced by the light of the moon.

"I really like," said Dad, "the runcible spoon." Reader, there are worse things to like. Or to love.

acknowledgments

T HANKS FIRST TO Tim Duggan, my editor, and Betsy Lerner, my agent, for their confidence in this peculiar project. I'm also grateful to many people at HarperCollins, each of whom was indispensable to the book in your hand. They are Jonathan Burnham, Doug Johnson, Katherine Beitner, Allison Lorentzen, Emily Cunningham, Leah Carlson-Stanisic, David Stanford Burr, Carla Jablonski, and Margaret Drislane. In addition, Fred Courtright at the Permissions Company helped a confused poetry critic obtain the rights for many of the poems reprinted here.

Two chapters of this book—"Ambition" and "The Political"—appeared in abridged form in, respectively, *The New York Times Book Review* and *Poetry*. Greg Cowles at the *Times* and Christian Wiman at *Poetry* edited those pieces.

acknowledgments

Michael Donohue, Maureen McLane, and James Richardson made extremely helpful comments on an early version of the manuscript (all subsequent errors and overstatements are my own). I'm grateful to Kristin Hanson for advice about form, and to Alan Cordle for his generous assistance with the archives of Foetry.com. I'm also indebted to Princeton University, where I began researching this book while a Hodder Fellow in 2006–7, and to my occasional compatriots at Trachtenberg Rodes & Friedberg.

Many other friends have patiently listened to me complain/brag/whine/dither through various stages of the writing and publication process over the past several years. I'd be remiss not to mention in particular Steven Bennett, Liz Camp, Sophie Gee, Lev Grossman, Jill North, Jessica Ratcliff, Ted Sider, Nico Silins, and Dmitri Tymoczko.

Finally, I'm grateful to Elaine Orr, Tripp and Susan Spann, and Steven and Annie Dixon. And my gratitude to Karen Bennett is the kind of thing you could write poems about.

index

3X LAD 7/12